Spurgeon's Sermons
on the
Second Coming

CONDENSED AND EDITED BY
DAVID OTIS FULLER, D.D.
Pastor, Wealthy Street Baptist Temple
Grand Rapids, Michigan

SECOND EDITION

ZONDERVAN PUBLISHING HOUSE
GRAND RAPIDS, MICHIGAN

EIGHT FORTY-SEVEN OTTAWA AVENUE
GRAND RAPIDS, MICHIGAN

PREFACE

THERE'S NO QUESTION about it; what William Shakespeare is to English prose, Charles Haddon Spurgeon is to the Christian pulpit. His superb and well nigh faultless diction, coupled with his burning love for Christ, make for him a niche in the Gospel ministry higher than all others since the days of the Apostle Paul.

We feel sure the reader will be delighted with this collection of sermons on the Second Coming of Christ by the great London preacher. He deals with this great and precious truth in a way that is at once sane, Scriptural and satisfying. For instance, read what he says in his message on "Behold, He Cometh With Clouds." "Brethren, no truth ought to be more frequently proclaimed, next to the first coming of the Lord, than His second coming; and you cannot thoroughly set forth all the ends and bearings of the first advent if you forget the second . . . All the prophets say that He will come. From Enoch down to the last that spoke by inspiration they declare, 'The Lord cometh with ten thousands of His saints' . . . If He came to die, doubt not that He will come to reign. If He came to be despised and rejected of men, why should we doubt that He will come to be admired in all them that believe?"

Mr. Spurgeon's sermon on "The First Resurrection" is, in the estimation of the writer of this preface, worth the price of the book alone. It is truly one of his masterpieces. To read these messages, straight from the heart of a man desperately in love with Jesus Christ, is to bring a new warmth and a new love in your life for this soon coming King of kings and Lord of lords.

DAVID OTIS FULLER

Grand Rapids, Michigan

CONTENTS

Chapter I

THE FIRST RESURRECTION

[Of this sermon the author makes mention, as one which had been used by the Spirit to bless the souls of men, both in the hearing and reading of it. It was delivered in his new Church Edifice, the Metropolitan Tabernacle, May 5, 1861. The doctrinal part of the discourse touches the much disputed question of the Millennium, and Christ's personal reign on earth. His spirit is kind, his discussion manly, and his practical inferences plain, earnest and solemn.]

"And I saw thrones, and they sat upon them, and judgment was given unto them: and I saw the souls of them that were beheaded for the witness of Jesus, and for the word of God, and which had not worshiped the beast, neither his image, neither had received his mark upon their foreheads, or in their hands; and they lived and reigned with Christ a thousand years. But the rest of the dead lived not again until the thousand years were finished. This is the first resurrection. Blessed and holy is he that hath part in the first resurrection; on such the second death hath no power, but they shall be priests of God and of Christ, and shall reign with him a thousand years" (Revelation 20:4-6).

"And I saw the dead, small and great, stand before God; and the books were opened; and another book was opened, which is the book of life; and the dead were judged out of those things which were written in the books, according to their works" (Revelation 20:12).

YOU WILL BEAR ME WITNESS, my friends, that it is exceedingly seldom I ever intrude into the mysteries of the future with regard either to the second advent, the millennial reign, or the first and second resurrection. As often as we come across it in our expositions, we

5

do not turn aside from the point, but if guilty at all on this point, it is rather in being too silent than saying too much.

And now, in bringing forward this question, I would say, I do not do it to amuse your curiosity by novelty, or that I may pretend to have the true key of the prophecies which are as yet unfulfilled. I scarcely think it would be justifiable for me to spend my time upon prophetic studies for which I have not the necessary talent, nor is it the vocation to which my Master has ordained me. I think some ministers would do far more for the profit of God's people, if they would preach more about the first advent and less about the second. But I have chosen this topic because I believe it has practical bearings, and may be made useful, instructive, and rousing to us all.

I find that the most earnest of the Puritanic preachers did not forbear to dwell upon this mysterious subject. I turn to Charnock; and in his disquisition upon the Immutability of God, he does not hesitate to speak of the conflagration of the world, of the millennial reign, and the new heavens and new earth.

I turn to Richard Baxter, a man who greatly loved the souls of men; who more perhaps than any man, with the exception of the apostle Paul, travailed in birth for souls; and I find him making a barbed arrow out of the doctrine of the coming of the Lord, and thrusting this great truth into the very heart and conscience of unbelievers, as though it were heaven's own sword.

John Bunyan too — plain, honest John — he who preached so simply that a child could comprehend him, and was certainly never guilty of having written upon his forehead the word "Mystery," he, too, speaks of the advent of Christ, and of the glories which shall follow; and uses this doctrine as a stimulus to the saints, and as a warning to the ungodly.

I do not think therefore I need tremble very much if the charge should be brought against me of bringing before you an unprofitable subject. It shall profit if God shall bless the word; and if it be God's Word we may expect His blessing if we preach it all, but He will withdraw it if we refrain from teaching any part of His council because in our pretended wisdom we fancy that it would not have practical effect.

I. We take the first text with its THREE PRIVILEGES. "Blessed and holy is he that hath part in the first resurrection: on such the second death hath no power, but they shall be priests of God and of Christ, and shall reign with him a thousand years."

Before I proceed to these privileges, I must remark that two modes of understanding this verse have been proposed, both of which I think are untenable. I have been reading carefully through Albert Barnes. He gives it, as his opinion, that the first resurrection here spoken of is a *resurrection of principles*—a resurrection of the patience, the undaunted courage, the holy boldness and constancy of the ancient martyrs. He says these great principles have been forgotten, and, as it were, buried; and that during the spiritual reign of Christ which is to come, these great principles will have a resurrection. ✗

Now, I appeal to you, would you, in reading that passage, think this to be the meaning? Would any man believe that to be its meaning, if he had not some thesis to defend? The fact is, we sometimes read Scripture, thinking of what it ought to say, rather than what it does say. I do not hesitate to affirm that any simple-minded person, who was intent upon discovering the mind of the Spirit, and not upon finding a method by which the words could be compelled to express his own mind, would say that the resurrection of principles, or the resurrection of doctrines, does not give the fair meaning of the words here stated.

Brethren, cannot you perceive at a glance that this is the resurrection of *men?* And is it not a literal resurrection, too? Does it not say, "I saw the souls of them that were beheaded for the witness of Jesus"? Is it not written, "The rest of the dead lived not"? Does this mean the rest of the dead principles? the rest of the dead doctrines? You cannot so translate it. It is—we have no doubt whatever—a literal resurrection of the saints of God, and not of principles nor of doctrines.

Brethren, the Holy Ghost does not jumble metaphors and facts together. A typical book has plain indications that it is so intended, and when you come upon a literal passage in a typical chapter, it is always attached to a something else which is distinctly literal, so that you cannot, without violence to common sense, make a typical meaning out of it.

The fact is, in reading this passage with an unbiased judgment, having no purpose whatever to serve, having no theory to defend—and I confess I have none, for I know but very little about mysteries to come—I could not help seeing there are *two literal resurrections* here spoken of, one of the spirits of the just, and the other of the bodies of the wicked; one of the saints who sleep in Jesus, whom God shall bring with *Him,* and another of those who live and die impenitent, who perish in their sins.

But this by way of preface. There are three privileges in the text.

1. Now the first privilege, *the priority of resurrection.* I think Scripture is exceedingly plain and explicit upon this point. You have perhaps imagined that all men will rise at the same moment; that the trump of the archangel will break open every grave at the same instant, and sound in the ear of every sleeper at the identical moment. Such I do not think is the testimony of the Word of God. I think the Word of God teaches, indisputably, that the saints shall rise first. And be the interval of time whatever it may, whether the thousand years are literal years, or a very long period of time, I am not now about to determine; I have nothing to do except with the fact that there are two resurrections, a resurrection of the just, and afterwards of the unjust— a time when the saints of God shall rise, an aftertime when the wicked shall rise to the resurrection of damnation.

I shall now refer you to one or two passages in Scripture, and you will use your Bibles and follow me. First, let us look at the words of the apostle in that chapter which we use generally as a burial service, the first epistle to the Corinthians, 15:20:—"But now is Christ risen from the dead, and become the first-fruits of them that slept. For since by man came death, by man came also the resurrection of the dead. For as in Adam all die, even so in Christ shall all be made alive. But every man in his own order: Christ the first-fruits; afterward they that are Christ's at his coming. Then cometh the end, when he shall have delivered up the kingdom to God, even the Father; when he shall have put down all rule and all authority and power."

There has been an interval of two thousand years between "Christ the firstfruits" and the "afterward they that are Christ's at his coming." Why not then a thousand years between that first resurrection and "the end"? Here is a resurrection of those who are Christ's, and of them only. As for the wicked, one would scarce know that they would rise at all from this passage, if it were not for the general statement, "All shall be made alive," and even this may not be so comprehensive as at first sight it seems. It is enough for me that there is here a particular and exclusive resurrection of those who are Christ's.

Turn to another passage, which is, perhaps, plainer still; the first epistle to the Thessalonians, 4:13:—"But I would not have you to be ignorant, brethren, concerning them which are asleep, that ye sorrow not, even as others which have no hope. For if we believe that Jesus died and rose again, even so them also which sleep in Jesus will God bring with him. For this we say unto you by the word of the Lord, that we which are alive and remain unto the coming of the Lord shall not prevent"—or have preference beyond—"them which are asleep. For the Lord himself shall descend from heaven with a shout, with the voice of the archangel, and with the trump of God: and the dead in Christ shall rise first: then we which are alive and remain shall be caught up together with them in the clouds, to meet the Lord in the air: and so shall we ever be with the Lord."

Here is nothing said whatever about the resurrection of the wicked; it is only stated that the dead in Christ shall rise first. Our apostle is evidently speaking of a first resurrection: and since we know that a first resurrection implies a second, and since we know that the wicked dead are to rise as well as the righteous dead, we draw the inference that the wicked dead shall rise at the second resurrection, after the interval between the two resurrections shall have been accomplished.

Turn to Philippians 3, verses 8 and 11, and compare the two. "Yea, doubtless, and I count all things but loss for the excellency of the knowledge of Christ Jesus my Lord; for whom I have suffered the loss of all things, and do count them but dung, that I may win Christ." "That I may know him, and the power of his resurrection, and the fellowship of his sufferings, being made conformable unto his death; if by any means I might attain unto the resurrection of the dead."

What does he mean there? Every one will rise; no orthodox Christian doubts that. The doctrine of a general resurrection is received by all the Christian Church. What, then, is this resurrection after which Paul was exerting himself, if by any means he might attain unto it? It could not be the general resurrection; he would attain unto that, live as he list. It must have been some superior resurrection, of which only those shall be partakers who have known Christ and the power of His resurrection, having been made conformable unto His death. I think you cannot interpret this passage, or give it any force of meaning, without you admit that there is to be a prior resurrection of the just, before the resurrection of the unjust.

If you will turn to a passage in Luke 20:35, which probably is fresh upon your memories, you will find there something which I will venture to call a clear proof of a special resurrection. The Sadducees had proposed a difficulty as to the relationship of men and women in the future state, and Jesus here says, "But they which shall be accounted worthy to obtain that world, and the resurrection from the dead, neither marry, nor are given in marriage: neither can they die any more: for they are equal unto the angels; and are the children of God, being the children of the resurrection."

Now, brethren, there is some *worthiness* necessary for this resurrection. Do you not perceive it? There is some distinction involved in being called the children of the resurrection. In that sense, then, every man would be one of the children of the resurrection; in that sense, no worthiness would be required for resurrection at all.

There must be, then, a resurrection for which worthiness is needed, a resurrection which shall be a distinguished privilege, which, being obtained, shall confer upon its possessor the distinguished and honorable title of a "child of the resurrection." It seems to me that this is plain enough, and can be put beyond all dispute.

In chapter 14 of the same gospel, in verse 14, you have a promise made to those who, when they make a feast, do not do it with the intention of getting anything in return. "When thou makest a feast, call the poor, the maimed, the lame, the blind: and thou shalt be blessed; for they cannot recompense thee: for thou shalt be recompensed at the resurrection of the just."

I would not insist upon it that this would prove that the just rose at a different time; but still there is to be a resurrection of the just, and on the other hand, there is to be a resurrection of the unjust; and the time of recompense for the righteous is to be the resurrection of the just, which is spoken of as being a particular period. He might just as well have said, "Thou shalt be recompensed at the general resurrection." There was no need to have said, "At the resurrection of the just," if the two are to happen at the same time. The words "of the just" are superfluous in the passage, unless they do refer to some era distinguished and distinct from the resurrection of the unjust.

I will not say that this is any clear proof, but still, all these put together, with other passages I might quote if time did not fail me, would, I think, establish upon a Scriptural basis the doctrine of the two resurrections.

But I would refer to one more, which seems to me to be exceedingly clear, in John 6:39, 40, 44, 54. In these verses the Saviour four times over speaks of His own believing people, and promises them a resurrection. "I will raise him up at the last day." Now, is there any joy or beauty in this, to the people of God in particular, unless there be a speciality in it for them? It is the lot of all to rise, and yet we have here a privilege for the elect! Surely, brethren, there is a different resurrection.

Besides, there is yet a passage which now springs to my memory in the Hebrews, where the apostle, speaking of the trials of the godly, and their noble endurance, speaks of them as "not accepting deliverance that they might obtain a better resurrection." The *betterness* was not in the after results of resurrection, but in the resurrection itself. How, then, could it be a better resurrection, unless there be some distinction between the resurrection of the saint and the resurrection of the sinner?

Let the one be a resurrection of splendor; let the

other be a resurrection of gloom and horror, and let there be a marked division between the two, that as it was in the beginning, it may be even to the end, the Lord hath put a difference between him that feareth God and him that feareth him not.

I am well aware that I have not been able to put the argument so well but that any antagonist may cavil at it; but I have been preaching to my own congregation rather than fighting with opponents, and I hope you will take these passages and weigh them for yourselves, and if they do not teach you that the dead in Christ shall rise first, do not believe me if I say they do. If you cannot perceive the fact yourself, if the Holy Spirit show it not unto you, why then read the passage again, and find if you can another and a better meaning.

I have no purpose to serve except to make the Scripture as plain to you as possible; and I say it yet again, I have not the shadow of a doubt in my own mind that these passages do teach us that there shall first of all be a resurrection concerning which it shall be said, "Blessed and holy is he that hath part in the first resurrection; on such the second death hath no power, but they shall be priests of God and of Christ, and shall reign with him a thousand years."

2. I now pass to the second privilege promised to the godly. *The second death on them hath no power.* This, too, is a literal death; none the less literal because its main terror is spiritual, for a spiritual death is as literal as a carnal death. The death which shall come upon the ungodly, without exception, can never touch the righteous.

Oh, brethren, this is the best of all. As for the first resurrection, if Christ hath granted that to His people,

there must be something glorious in it if we cannot
perceive it. "It doth not yet appear what we shall be,
but we know when he shall appear we shall be like
him." I think the glories of the first resurrection belong
to the glories which shall be revealed *in* us rather than
to the glories that are revealed *to* us. What shall be
the majesty of that form in which we shall rise, what
the distinguished happiness we shall then enjoy, we can
but guess at a distance, we cannot know it to the full.

But on this point we can understand what Scripture
states, and understand this much well, that damnation,
the second death, shall have no power on those who
rise at the first resurrection. How should it? How can
damnation fall on any but those who are sinners and
are guilty of sin? But the saints are not guilty of sin.
They have sinned like others, and they were by nature
the children of wrath even as others. But their sin has
been lifted from them: it was laid upon the scapegoat's
head of old.

He, the Eternal substitute, even our Lord Jesus, carried
all their guilt and their iniquity into the wilderness of
forgetfulness, where it shall never be found against
them forever. They wear the Saviour's righteousness,
even as they have been washed in His blood; and what
wrath can lie on the man who is not only guiltless
through the blood, but is meritorious through imputed
righteousness!

Oh, arm of Justice, thou art nerveless to smite the
blood-washed! Oh, ye flames of hell, how could even
so much as the breath of your heat pass upon the man
who is safe covered in the Saviour's wounds! How is
it possible for you, O Deaths, Destructions, Horrors,
Glooms, Plagues, and Terrors, so much as to flit over

the serene sky of the spirit which has found peace with
God through the blood of Christ!

There shall be a second death; but over us it shall
have no power. Do you understand the beauty of the
picture? As if we might walk through the flames of
hell and they should have *no power* to devour us any
more than when the holy children walked with ease
over the hot coals of Nebuchadnezzar's seven times
heated furnace.

Death may bend his bow and fit the arrow to the
string. But we laugh at thee, O Death! and thee, O
hell, we will despise! for over both of you, ye enemies
of man, we shall be more than conquerors through
Him that hath loved us. We shall stand invulnerable
and invincible, defying and laughing to scorn every foe.
And all this because we are washed from sin and
covered with a spotless righteousness.

But there is another reason why the second death
can have no power on the believer; because, when the
prince of this world cometh against us, then we shall
be able to say what our Master did, "He hath nothing
in me." When we shall rise again, we shall be freed
from all corruption; no evil tendencies shall remain in
us. "I will cleanse their blood that I have not cleansed
—for the Lord dwelleth in Zion."

"Without spot or wrinkle, or any such thing," without even the shadow of a spot which the eye of Om-
niscience could discover, we shall be as pure as Adam
before his fall, as holy as the Immaculate manhood
when it first came from the divine hand. We shall be
better than Adam, for Adam might sin, but we shall
be so established in goodness, in truth, and in righteousness, that we shall not even be tempted again, much

less shall we have any fear of falling. We shall stand spotless and faultless at the last great day.

Brethren, lift up your heads. Contending with sin, cast down with doubts, lift up your heads, and wipe the tears from your eyes. There are days coming, the like of which angels have not seen, but you shall see them. There are times coming when your spirits shall no more fear the chain, nor shall ye even remember the wormwood and the gall. And when they rise they shall leave the old Adam behind them. Blessed day! One of the most blessed parts of heaven—of heaven above or of heaven below—will be freedom from the tendency to sin, a total death to that old nature which has been our plague and woe.

3. The third privilege of the text is, *"They shall reign with him a thousand years."* Here is another point upon which there has been a long and vigorous contention. It was believed in the early Church, (I do not know whether there is any Scriptural foundation for the precise date they fixed), that the seventh thousand years of the world's history would be a Sabbath; that, as there were six days of toil in the week, and the seventh was a day of rest, so the world would have six thousand years of toil and sorrow, and the seventh thousand would be a thousand years of rest.

I say I do not know that there is any Scripture for that; I do know that there is none against it. I believe the Lord Himself shall come, "but of that day and of that hour knoweth no man, no, not even the angels of God." And I think it is idle to attempt to fix the year or even the century, when Christ shall come. Our business is to expect Him always, to be always looking for His appearing, watching for His coming; that

whether He come at cock-crow, or midnight, or at
morning watch, we may be ready to go in with the
wise virgins to the marriage feast, and rejoice with our
Beloved. If there have been any dates given, I am not
able at present to find them out. All these dates and
mysteries I can leave to much more learned men, and
men who give their whole time to it.

The book of Revelation needs another expounder besides those who have loaded our shelves until they
groan, for they have generally made confusion worse
confounded. Their expositions have been rather "an
obvelation" than a revelation; they have rather darkened
counsel by words without knowledge, than made the
dark things plain.

I am prepared to go about as far as my predecessor,
Dr. Gill went; as far as the old fathers of the Church
went; as far as Baxter and Bunyan would have gone,
but to go no further than that. Yet I think we may say
this morning, there is in the text a distinct promise that
the saints are to reign with Christ a thousand years;
and I believe they are to reign with Him *upon this
earth*.

There are some passages which I think obtain a
singular fulness of meaning if this be true. Turn to
Psalm 37:10, 11. It is that Psalm where David has
been fretting himself, because of the evil doers, and
their prosperity upon the earth. He says, "For yet a
little while, and the wicked shall not be: yea, thou
shalt diligently consider his place, and it shall not be.
But the meek shall inherit the earth; and shall delight
themselves in the abundance of peace." You can interpret that to mean that the meek man shall enjoy

much more of this world's goods than the sinner, and that he shall have abundance of peace.

But I think you have given it a lean meaning, a very lean meaning, indeed. If it be true that these meek ones shall yet possess this very earth, and that here, in the abundance of peace through the Messiah's reign, they shall rejoice in it, I think you have found a fuller meaning, and one which is more like God's promises.

So it is that God's promises always have a wider meaning than we can conceive; now, in this case, if it only mean that the meek are to have what they gain in this life, which is very little indeed, if they are only to have what they enjoy here upon earth, which is so little, that I think if in this life only they have hope, they are of men the most miserable—if it only mean that, then the promise means less than we might conceive it to mean.

But if it mean that they shall have glory even here, then you have given to it one of the widest meanings you can conceive, a meaning like the promises of God— wide, extensive, and worthy of Himself. Brethren, the meek do not inherit the earth to any great degree at present, and we look for this in another age. Let me quote the language of Christ, lest you should think this passage peculiar to the Old Testament dispensation, "Blessed are the meek, for they shall inherit the earth." How? where? when? Not now certainly, not in Christ's days, not in apostolic times, by any means. What did the meek inherit, brethren? Faggot, flames, racks, pincers, dungeons. Their inheritance, indeed, was nothing. They were destitute, afflicted, tormented; they wandered about in sheepskins and goatskins; and if the meek are

ever to inherit the earth, certainly it must be in some
age to come, for they have never inherited it yet.

Turn again to a passage in Revelation, 5:9, 10: "And
they sung a new song." It is the very song we sang
this morning, and it runs thus: "Thou art worthy to
take the book, and to open the seals thereof: for thou
wast slain, and hast redeemed us to God by thy blood
out of every kindred, and tongue, and people, and
nation; and hast made us unto our God kings and
priests: and we shall reign *on the earth*."

Whether any one disputes the genuineness of these
words, I do not know; but if they mean anything at
all, if the Holy Spirit means to set forth any meaning,
surely it must have been that the people of Christ
shall reign upon the earth. Besides, remember our
Saviour's words in Matthew 19:28, where, in answer to
a question which had been put by Peter, as to what
His saints should have as the result of their losses for
His sake, He said unto them, "Verily I say unto you,
that ye which have followed me in the regeneration,
when the Son of man shall sit in the throne of his
glory, ye also shall sit upon twelve thrones, judging
the twelve tribes of Israel. And every one that hath
forsaken houses, or brethren, or sisters, or father, or
mother, or wife, or children, or lands, for my name's
sake, shall receive an hundredfold, and shall inherit
everlasting life."

It seems that Christ here is to come in the regeneration, when in a new-born world there shall be joys
fitted for the newborn spirits; and then there shall be
splendors and glories for the apostles first, and for all
those who by any means have suffered any losses for
Christ Jesus.

You find such passages as these in the Word of God: "The Lord of Hosts shall reign in Mount Zion, and in Jerusalem, and before his ancients gloriously." You find another like this in Zechariah, "My God shall come with the multitude of his saints." Indeed, I could not now take up your time by quoting many passages in which it seems to me that nothing but the triumph on the very spot where they have fought the battle, nothing but the glory in the very place where they have had the tug of war, will meet the meaning of God's Word.

I do look forward to this with joy, that though I may sleep in Christ before my Master come, and I know not whether that shall be or no, yet I shall rise at the day of His appearing, and shall be recompensed at the resurrection of the just, if I have truly and faithfully served Him; and that recompense shall be, to be made like unto Him, and to partake of His glories before the eyes of men, and to reign with Him during the thousand years.

But, to make one other observation. This doctrine which I have preached just now is not an unpractical one. For throughout the New Testament, whenever the apostle wants to stir up men to patience, to labor, to hope, to endurance, to holiness, he generally says something about the advent of Christ. "Be patient, brethren," says he, "for the coming of the Lord draweth nigh." "Let your moderation be known unto all men, the Lord is at hand." "Judge nothing before the time, till the Lord come." "When the great Shepherd shall appear, ye also shall appear with him in glory."

Brethren, I think we shall do wrong if we make too much of this; but we shall do equally wrong if we

make too little of it. Let us give it a fair place in our
thoughts, and especially let those of us who fear God
and believe in Jesus, take this to be a window through
which we can look, when the house is dark and our
home is full of misery; let us look to the time when
we shall rise among the first, following Christ the
firstfruits, when we shall reign with Christ, sharing in
His glories, and when we shall know that the second
death over us hath no power.

II. I shall now turn to the second part of the discourse briefly. To the ungodly, THREE THINGS IN
SIMPLICITY.

Sinner, you have heard us speak of the resurrection
of the righteous. To you the word "resurrection" has
no music. There is no flash of joy in your spirit when
you hear that the dead shall rise again. But oh, I pray
thee lend me thine ear while I assure thee in God's
name that thou shalt rise. Not only shall your soul
live—you have perhaps become so brutish that you
forget you have a soul—but your body itself shall live.

Those eyes that have been full of lust shall see sights
of horror; those ears which have listened to the temptations of the evil one, shall hear the thunders of the
day of judgment; those very feet that bare you to the
theater, shall attempt, but utterly fail to sustain you
when Christ shall sit in judgment. Think not when
your body is put into the sail that you have done with
it. It has been partner with your soul in sin; it shall be
sharer with your soul in the punishment. He is able to
cast both body and soul into hell.

The heathens believed in the immortality of the soul.
We need not therefore prove what a heathen could
conceive. It is the doctrine of the resurrection of the

body which is peculiar to Christianity. You are not prepared to cast away the revelation of God I know. You receive that book as being God's book, and it tells me that all the dead, both small and great, shall rise.

When the archangel's trump shall sound, the old inhabitants of the world before the flood shall rise out of the ocean. The buried palaces, the sunken homes, shall all give up the multitude who once married and were given in marriage, until Noah entered into the ark. Up shall rise from the great deeps of the fathomless sea, thousands upon thousands of men who have slept now these three and four thousand years. Every churchyard, too, where men have been quietly buried with Christian rites, but yet were unchristian still, shall yield up its dead.

The battlefield shall yield a mighty harvest, a harvest which was sown in blood, and which shall be reaped in tempest. Every place where man has lived and man has died shall see the dying quickened once again, and flesh and blood once more instinct with life.

But the main thing with you is that *you* will be there. Living and dying as you now are, ungodly and unconverted, the most awful curse that could fall on you, with the exception of the damnation of your soul, is the sure and certain resurrection of your body. Go, now, and paint it if you will, and seek a beauty which the worm shall loathe. Go and pamper your body; drink the sweet and eat the fat. Go and luxuriate and indulge in ease. Oh, sir, you may well pamper your bodies, for there is short enough time for your body to have mirth; and when that short time is over thou shalt drink another wine—the dregs of the cup of

God's wrath, which the wicked shall drain to the last drop.

Satisfy thine ears with music now; thou shalt soon hear nothing but the howling of the damned! Go thou thy way, eat, drink, and be merry; but for all these the Lord shall bring thee into judgment—sevenfold for all thy sinful pleasures, yea seventy times seven, for all thy joys of lust, and wickedness and crime, shall the Lord be avenged on thee, in the great and terrible day of His wrath. Sinner, think thou of this, and when thou sinnest think of the resurrection.

But after the resurrection, according to the text, comes *the judgment.* You have cursed God. The oath died away. No, sir, it did not; it imprinted itself upon the great book of God's remembrance. You have entered the chamber of wantonness, or the hall of infidelity; you have walked through the stews of crime, and through the stench and filth of the brothel; you have wandered into sin and plunged into it, thinking it would all die with the day.

Not so. The books shall be opened. I think I see you with your blanching cheeks, closing your eyes because you dare not look upon the Judge when He opens that page where stands your history. I hear yon sinner, boldest among you all. He is crying, "Ye rocks fall on me." There they stand, sublime and dread, those granite rocks; he would rather be crushed than stand there before the avenging eye; but the mountains will not loosen, their flinty bowels feel no pangs of sympathy, they will not move. You stand while the fiery eye looks you through and through, and the dread voice reads on, and on, and on, your every act, and word, and thought.

I see you as the shameful crime is read, and men and angels hear. I see your horror as a nameless deed is told, in terms explicit, which none can misunderstand. I hear your thoughts brought out—that lust, that murder which was in the thought, but never grew into the deed. And you are all this while astonished like Belshazzar, when he saw the writing on the wall and his loins were loose, and he was terribly afraid. So shall it be with you; and yet again, and again, and again, shall you send up that awful shriek, "Hide us! hide us from the face of him that sitteth upon the throne, and from the wrath of the Lamb!"

But then cometh the end. After death the judgment; after judgment *the damnation*. If it be a dreadful thing to live again, if it be a more dreadful thing still to spend the first day of that life in the grand assize of God, how much more awful shall it be when the sentence is pronounced, and the terror of punishment shall begin!

We believe that the souls of the wicked are already tormented, but this judgment will cast both body and soul into the lake of fire. Men and women, ye who fear not God, and have no faith in Jesus, I cannot picture to you damnation. Across it let me draw a curtain. But though we must not picture it, I pray you realize it. When Martin has painted some of his sublime pictures, he has generally heightened the effect by masses of darkness. Surely, this is the way in which God has painted hell, rather by masses of darkness than by definiteness of light.

This much we know, that hell is a place of absence from God—a place for the development of sin, where every passion is unbridled, every lust unrestrained—a

place where God punishes night and day those who
sin night and day—a place where there is never sleep,
or rest, or hope—a place where a drop of water is
denied, though thirst shall burn the tongue—a place
where pleasure never breathed, where light never
dawned, where anything like consolation was never
heard of—a place where the gospel is denied, where
mercy droops her wings and dies—a place where vengeance reigns, shakes his chains, and brandishes his
sword—a place of fury and of burning, a place the
like of which imagination hath not pictured.

May God grant it may be a place which you shall
never see, and whose dread you shall never feel. Sinner,
instead of preaching it thee, let me bid thee fly from it.
Die, sinner, and flight from hell becomes impossible;
thou art lost, then, eternally. Oh, while yet thou art
on praying ground, I pray thee, think on thy end.
Think! think! this warning may be the last you shall
ever hear. You may never be spared to come to a place
of worship again. Perhaps, while you sit here, the
last sands are dropping from the hour glass; and then,
no more warning can be given, because redemption
and escape shall be impossible to you.

Soul, I lift up before thee, Christ the crucified one—
"Whosoever believeth on Him shall never perish, but
hath eternal life." As Moses lifted up the serpent in
the wilderness, so this morning the Son of Man is lifted
up. Sinner, see His wounds. Look to His thorn-crowned
head. See the nails of His hands and of His feet. Do
you perceive Him? Hark! while He cries, "Why hast
thou forsaken me?" Listen again, while He says, "It
is finished! It is finished!" Salvation finished! And
now, salvation is freely preached to thee. Believe on

Christ and thou shalt be saved. Trust Him, and all the horrors of the future shall have no power over you; but the splendors of this prophecy shall be fulfilled, be they what they may.

Oh, that this morning some of you may trust my Master for the first time in your lives; and this done, you need not curiously enquire what the future shall be, but you may sit down calmly and say, "Come when it will; my soul is on the rock of ages; it fears no ill; it fears no tempest; it defies all pain. Come quickly! come quickly! even so, come quickly, Lord Jesus." AMEN.

Chapter II

THE WATCHWORD FOR TODAY:
"STAND FAST"

"For our conversation is in heaven; from whence also we look for the Saviour, the Lord Jesus Christ: who shall change our vile body, that it may be fashioned like unto His glorious body, according to the working whereby he is able to subdue all things unto himself. Therefore, my brethren dearly beloved and longed for, my joy and crown, so stand fast in the Lord, my dearly beloved" (Philippians 3:20, 21; 4:1).

EVERY DOCTRINE of the Word of God has its practical bearing. As each tree beareth seed after its kind, so doth every truth of God bring forth practical virtues. Hence you find the apostle Paul very full of *therefores* —his therefores being the conclusions drawn from certain statements of divine truth. I marvel that our excellent translators should have divided the argument from the conclusion by making a new chapter where there is least reason for it.

Last Lord's day I spoke with you concerning the most sure and certain resurrection of our Lord Jesus: now there is a practical force in that truth, which constitutes part of what is meant by "the power of his resurrection." Since the Lord has risen, and will surely come a second time, and will raise the bodies of His people at His coming, there is something to wait for, and a grand reason for steadfastness while thus waiting. We are looking for the coming of our Lord and Saviour

Jesus Christ from heaven, and that He shall "fashion anew the body of our humiliation, that it may be conformed to the body of His glory"; therefore let us stand fast in the position which will secure us this honor. Let us keep our posts until the coming of the great Captain shall release the sentinels.

The glorious resurrection will abundantly repay us for all the toil and travail we may have to undergo in the battle for the Lord. The glory to be revealed even now casts a light upon our path, and causes sunshine within our hearts. The hope of this happiness makes us even now strong in the Lord, and in the power of His might.

Paul was deeply anxious that those in whom he had been the means of kindling the heavenly hope might be preserved faithful until the coming of Christ. He trembled lest any of them should seem to draw back, and prove traitors to their Lord. He dreaded lest he should lose what he hoped he had gained, by their turning aside from the faith. Hence he beseeches them to "stand fast." He expressed in the sixth verse of the first chapter his conviction that He who had begun a good work in them would perform it, but his intense love made him exhort them, saying, "Stand fast in the Lord, my dearly beloved." By such exhortations final perseverance is promoted and secured.

Paul has fought bravely; and in the case of the Philippian converts he believes that he has secured the victory, and he fears lest it should yet be lost. He reminds me of the death of that British hero, Wolfe, who on the heights of Quebec received a mortal wound. It was just at the moment when the enemy fled, and when he knew that they were running, a smile was on his face, and he cried, "Hold me up. Let not my brave soldiers see me drop. The day is ours. Oh, do keep it!" His sole anxiety was to make the victory sure.

Thus warriors die, and thus Paul lived. His very soul seems to cry, "We have won the day. Oh, do keep it!" O my beloved hearers, I believe that many of you are "in the Lord," but I entreat you to "stand fast in the Lord." In your case, also, the day is won; but oh, do keep it! There is the pith of all I have to say to you this morning: may God the Holy Spirit write it on your hearts! Having done all things well hitherto, I entreat you to obey the injunction of Jude, to keep "yourselves in the love of God," and to join with me in adoring Him who alone is able to keep us from falling, and to present us faultless before His presence with exceeding great joy. Unto Him be glory for ever. Amen.

I. Paul joyfully perceived that HIS BELOVED CONVERTS WERE IN THEIR RIGHT PLACE. It is a very important thing indeed that we should begin well. The start is not everything, but it is a great deal. It has been said by the old proverb, that "Well begun is half done"; and it is certainly so in the things of God. It is vitally important to enter in at the strait gate; to start on the heavenly journey from the right point. I have no doubt that many slips and falls and apostasies among professors are due to the fact that they were not right at first; the foundation was always upon the sand, and when the house came down at last, it was no more than might have been expected. A flaw in the foundation is pretty sure to be followed by a crack in the super-structure. Do see to it that you lay a good foundation. It is even better to have no repentance than a repentance which needs to be repented of: it is better to have no faith than a false faith: it is better to make no profession of religion than to make an untruthful one.

God give us grace that we may not make a mistake in learning the alphabet of godliness, or else in all our learning we shall blunder on and increase in error. We should early learn the difference between grace and merit, between the purpose of God and the will of man, between trust in God and confidence in the flesh. If we do not start aright, the further we go the further we shall be from our desired end, and the more thoroughly in the wrong shall we find ourselves. Yes, it is of prime importance that our new birth and our first love should be genuine beyond all question.

The only position, however, in which we can begin aright is to be "in the Lord." This is to begin as we may safely go on. This is the essential point. It is a very good thing for Christians to be in the church; but if you are in the church before you are in the Lord you are out of place. It is a good thing to be engaged in holy work; if you are in holy work before you are in the Lord you will have no heart for it, neither will the Lord accept it.

It is not essential that you should be in this church or in that church; but it is essential that you should be "in the Lord": it is not essential that you should be in the Sabbath-school, nor in the Working Meeting, nor in the Tract Society; but it is essential to the last degree that you should be in the Lord. The apostle rejoiced over those that were converted at Philippi because he knew that they were in the Lord. They were where he wished them to remain, therefore he said, "Stand fast in the Lord."

What is it to be "in the Lord"? Well, brethren, *we are in the Lord vitally and evidently when we fly to the Lord Jesus by repentance and faith,* and make Him to be our refuge and hiding-place. Is it so with you? Have you fled out of self? Are you trusting in the Lord alone? Have you come to Calvary, and beheld your Saviour? As the doves build their nests in the rock, have you thus made your home in Jesus? There is no shelter for a guilty soul but in His wounded side. Have you come there?

Are you in Him? Then keep there. You will never have a better refuge; in fact, there is no other. No other name is given under heaven among men whereby we must be saved. I cannot tell you to stand fast in the Lord, unless you are there: hence my enquiry is—Are you in Christ? Is He your only confidence? In His life, His death, and His resurrection do you find the grounds of your hope? Is He Himself all your salvation, and all your desire? If so, stand fast in Him.

Next, these people, in addition to having fled to Christ for refuge, were now *in Christ as to their daily life.* They had heard Him say, "Abide in Me"; and therefore they remained in the daily enjoyment of Him, in reliance upon Him, in obedience to Him, and in the earnest copying of His example. They were Christians, that is to say, persons upon whom was named the name of Christ. They were endeavoring to realize the power of His death and resurrection as a sanctifying influence, killing their sins and fostering their virtues. They were laboring to reproduce His image in themselves, that so they might bring glory to His name. Their lives were spent within the circle of their Saviour's influence.

Are you so, my dear friends? Then stand fast. You will never find a nobler example; you will never be saturated with a diviner spirit than that of Christ Jesus your Lord. Whether we eat or drink, or whatsoever we do, let us do all in the name of the Lord Jesus, and so live in Him.

This expression is very short, but very full. "In Christ." Does it not mean that we are in Christ as the birds are in the air which buoys them up, and enables them to fly? Are we not in Christ as the fish are in the sea? *Our Lord has become our element,* vital, and all surrounding. Has Jesus brought you into His green pastures? Then lie down in them. Go no further, for you will never fare better. Stay with your Lord, however long the night, for only in Him have you hope of morning.

You see, then, that these people were where they should be—in the Lord, and that this was the reason why the apostle took such delight in them. Kindly read the first verse of the fourth chapter, and see how he loves them, and joys over them. He heaps up titles of love! Some dip their morsel in vinegar, but Paul's words were saturated with honey.

Here we not only have sweet words, but they mean something: his love was real and fervent. The very heart of Paul is written out large in this verse—"Therefore, my brethren dearly beloved and longed for, my joy and crown, so stand fast in the Lord, my dearly beloved." Because they were in Christ, therefore first of all they were Paul's *brethren.* This was a new relationship, not earthly, but heavenly.

What did this Jew from Tarsus know about the Philippians? Many of them were Gentiles. Time was

when he would have called them dogs, and despised
them as the uncircumcised; but now he says, "My
brethren." That poor word has become very hackneyed.
We talk of brethren without particularly much of
brotherly love; but true brothers have a love for one
another which is very unselfish and admirable, and so
there is between real Christians a brotherhood which
they will neither disown, nor dissemble, nor forget.

It is said of our Lord, "For this cause He is not
ashamed to call them brethren"; and surely they need
never be ashamed to call one another brethren. Paul,
at any rate, looks at the jailor, that jailor who had set
his feet in the stocks, and he looks at the jailor's family,
and at Lydia, and many others; in fact, at the whole
company that he had gathered at Philippi, and he
salutes them lovingly as "My brethren." Their names
were written in the same family register because they
were in Christ, and therefore had one Father in heaven.

Next, the apostle calls them "my *dearly beloved*."
The verse almost begins with this word, and it quite
finishes with it. The repetition makes it mean, "My
doubly dear ones." Such is the love which every true
servant of Christ will have for those who have been
begotten to the faith of Christ by his means. Oh, yes,
if you are in Christ His ministers must love you. How
could there be a lack of affection in our hearts toward
you, since we have been the means of bringing you
to Jesus? Without cant or display we call you our
"dearly beloved."

Then the apostle calls them his *"longed for,"* that
is, his most desired ones. He first desired to see them
converted; after that he desired to see them baptized;
then he desired to see them exhibiting all the graces

of Christians. When he saw holiness in them he desired to visit them and commune with them. Their constant kindness created in him a strong desire to speak with them face to face. He loved them, and desired their company, because they were in Christ. So he speaks of them as those for whom he longed. His delight was in thinking of them and in hoping to visit them.

Then he adds, "My joy and crown." Paul had been the means of their salvation, and when he thought of that blessed result he never regretted all that he had suffered: his persecutions among the Gentiles seemed light indeed since these priceless souls were his reward. Though he was nothing but a poor prisoner of Christ, yet he talks in right royal style: they are his crown. They were his *stephanos,* or crown given as a reward for his life-race. This among the Greeks was usually a wreath of flowers placed around the victor's brow.

Paul's crown would never fade. He writes as he felt the amaranth around his temples; even now he looks upon the Philippians as his chaplet of honor: they were his joy and his crown; he anticipated, I do not doubt, that throughout eternity it would be a part of his heaven to see them amid their blessedness, and to know that he helped to bring them to that felicity by leading them to Christ.

O beloved, it is indeed our highest joy that we have not run in vain, neither labored in vain: you who have been snatched as "brands from the burning," and are now living to the praise of our Lord Jesus Christ, you are our prize, our crown, our joy.

These converts were all this to Paul simply because they were "in Christ." They had begun well, they were where they should be, and he therefore rejoiced in them.

II. But secondly, it was for this reason that HE
LONGED THAT THEY SHOULD KEEP THERE. He entreated
them to stand fast. "So stand fast in the Lord, my
dearly beloved." The beginning of religion is not the
whole of it. You must not suppose that the sum godliness is contained within the experience of a day or
two, or a week, or a few months, or even a few years.
Precious are the feelings which attend conversion; but
dream not that repentance, faith, and so forth, are for
a season, and then all is done, and done with.

I am afraid there are some who secretly say, "Everything is now complete; I have experienced the necessary
change, I have been to see the elders and the pastor,
and I have been baptized, and received into the church,
and now all is right for ever." That is a false view
of your condition. In conversion you have started in
the race, and you must run to the end of the course.
In your confession of Christ you have carried your tools
into the vineyard, but the day's work now begins. Remember, "He that shall endure unto the end, the same
shall be saved." Godliness is a life-long business. The
working out of the salvation which the Lord Himself
works in you is not a matter of certain hours, and of
a limited period of life. Salvation is unfolded throughout all our sojourn here. We continue to repent and
to believe, and even the process of our conversion con-
tinues as we are changed more and more into the image
of our Lord. Final perseverance is the necessary evidence
of genuine conversion.

In proportion as we rejoice over converts we feel
an intense bitterness when any disappoint us, and turn
out to be merely temporary camp-followers. We sigh
over the seed which springs up so speedily, but which

withers so soon because it has neither root nor depth of earth. We were ready to say—"Ring the bells of heaven"; but the bells of heaven did not ring because these people talked about Christ, and said they were in Christ; but it was all a delusion. After a while, for one reason and another, they went back; "they went out from us, but they were not of us; for if they had been of us, they would no doubt have continued with us: but they went out, that they might be made manifest that they were not all of us."

Our churches suffer most seriously from the great numbers who drop out of their ranks, and either go back to the world, or else must be pursuing a very secret and solitary path in their way to heaven, for we hear no more of them. Our joy is turned to disappointment, our crown of laurel becomes a circle of faded leaves, and we are weary at the remembrance of it. With what earnestness, therefore, would we say to you who are beginning the race, "Continue in your course. We beseech you turn not aside, neither slacken your running, till you have won the prize!"

I heard an expression yesterday which pleased me much. I spoke about the difficulty of keeping on. "Yes," answered my friend, "and it is harder still to keep on keeping on." So it is. There is the pinch. I know lots of fellows who are wonders at the start. What a rush they make! But then there is no stay in them: they soon lose breath. The difference between the spurious and the real Christian lies in this staying power. The real Christian has a life within him which can never die, an incorruptible seed which liveth and abideth for ever; but the spurious Christian begins after a fashion, but ends almost as soon as he begins. He is esteemed

a saint; but turns out a hypocrite. He makes a fair
show for a while, but soon he quits the way of holiness,
and makes his own damnation sure. God save you,
dear friends, from any thing which looks like apostasy.
Hence I would with all my might press upon you these
two most weighty words: "Stand fast."

I will put the exhortation thus—"Stand fast *doctrinally.*" In this age all the ships in the waters are pulling
up their anchors; they are drifting with the tide; they
are driven about with every wind. It is your wisdom
to put down more anchors. I have taken the precaution
to cast four anchors out of the stern, as well as to see
that the great bower anchor is in its proper place. I
will not budge an inch from the old doctrine for any
man.

Now that the cyclone is triumphant over many a
bowing wall and tottering fence, those who are built
upon the one foundation must prove its value by standing fast. We will hearken to no teaching but that of
the Lord Jesus. If you see a truth to be in God's
Word, grasp it by your faith; and if it be unpopular,
grapple it to you as with hooks of steel. If you are
despised as a fool for holding it, hold it the more.
Like an oak, take deeper root, because the winds would
tear you from your place. Defy reproach and ridicule,
and you have already vanquished it.

Stand fast, like the British squares in the olden times.
When fierce assaults were made upon them every man
seemed transformed to rock. We might have wandered
from the ranks a little in more peaceful times, to look
after the fascinating flowers which grow on every side
of our march; but, now we know that the enemy sur-
rounds us, we keep strictly to the line of march, and

tolerate no roaming. The watchword of the host of God just now is—"Stand fast!" Hold you to the faith once delivered to the saints. Hold fast the form of sound words, and deviate not one jot or tittle therefrom. Doctrinally stand fast!

Practically, also, abide firm in the right, the true, the holy. This is of the utmost importance. The barriers are broken down; they would amalgamate church and world: yes, even church and stage. It is proposed to combine God and devil in one service; Christ and Belial are to perform on one stage.

Surely now is the time when the lion shall eat straw like the ox, and very dirty straw too. So they say; but I repeat to you this word, "Come out from among them and be ye separate, and touch not the unclean thing." Write "holiness unto the Lord" not only on your altars, but upon the bells of the horses; let everything be done as before the living God. Do all things unto holiness and edification. Strive together to maintain the purity of the disciples of Christ; and take up your cross, and go without the camp bearing His reproach.

If you have already stood apart in your decision for the Lord, continue to do so. Stand fast. In nothing moved by the laxity of the age, in nothing affected by the current modern opinion, say to yourself, "I will do as Christ bids me to the utmost of my ability. I will follow the Lamb whithersoever He goeth." In these times of worldliness, impurity, self-indulgence, and error, it becomes the Christian to gather up his skirts and keep his feet and his garments clean from the pollution which lies all around him. We must be more

Puritanic and precise than we have been. Oh, for grace
to stand fast!

Mind also that you stand fast *experimentally*. Pray
that your inward experience may be a close adhesion to
your Master. Do not go astray from His presence.
Neither climb with those who dream of perfection in
the flesh, nor grovel with those who doubt the possibility
of present salvation. Take the Lord Jesus Christ to be
your sole treasure, and let your heart be ever with Him.

Stand fast in faith in His atonement, in confidence
in His Divinity, in assurance of His Second Advent. I
pine to know within my soul the power of His resurrection, and to have unbroken fellowship with Him. In
communion with the Father and the Son let us stand
fast. He shall fare well whose heart and soul, affections and understanding are wrapped up in Christ Jesus,
and in none beside. Concerning your inward life, your
secret prayer, your walk with God, here is the watchword of the day—"Stand fast."

Next, stand fast *without wavering in our trust*. Per-
mit no doubt to worry you. Know that Jesus can save
you, and, what is more, know that He has saved you.
So commit yourself to His hands, that you are as sure
of your salvation as of your existence. The blood of
Jesus Christ this day cleanseth us from all sin; His
righteousness covers us, and His life quickens us into
newness of life. Tolerate no doubt, mistrust, suspicion,
or misgiving. Believe in Christ up to the hilt. As for
myself, I will yield to be lost for ever if Jesus does
not save me. I will have no other string to my bow,
no second door of hope, or way of retreat. I could
risk a thousand souls on my Lord's truth and feel no

risk. Stand fast, without wishing for another trust, and without wavering in the trust you have.

Moreover, stand fast *without wandering into sin*. You are tempted this way and that way: stand fast. Inward passions rise: lusts of the flesh rebel; the devil hurls his fearful suggestions; the men of your own household tempt you: stand fast. Only so will you be preserved from the torrents of iniquity. Keep close to the example and spirit of your Master; and having done all, still stand.

As I have said, stand fast without wandering, so next I must say stand fast *without wearying*. You are a little tired. Never mind, take a little rest and brush up again. "Oh," you say, "this toil is so monotonous." Do it better, and that will be a change. Your Saviour endured His life and labor without this complaint, for zeal had eaten Him up.

"Alas!" you cry, "I cannot see results." Never mind; wait for results, even as the husbandman waiteth for the precious fruits of the earth. "Oh, sir, I plod along and make no progress." Never mind, you are a poor judge of your own success. Work on, for in due season you shall reap if you faint not. Practice perseverance.

Remember that if you have the work of faith and the labor of love, you must complete the trio by adding the patience of hope. You cannot do without this last. "Be ye stedfast, unmoveable, always abounding in the work of the Lord, forasmuch as ye know that your labor is not in vain in the Lord." I am reminded of Sir Christopher Wren, when he cleared away old St. Paul's to make room for his splendid pile. He was compelled to use battering rams upon the massive walls. The workmen kept on battering and battering. An enor-

mous force was brought to bear upon the walls for
days and nights, but it did not appear to have made
the least impression upon the ancient masonry. Yet
the great architect knew what he was at: he bade them
keep on incessantly, and the ram fell again and again
upon the rocky wall, till at length the whole mass was
disintegrating and coming apart; and then each stroke
began to tell. At a blow it reeled, at another it quivered,
at another it moved visibly, at another it fell over
amid clouds of dust.

These last strokes did the work. Do you think so?
No, it was the combination of blows, the first as truly
as the last. Keep on with the battering-ram. I hope
to keep on until I die. And, mark you, I may die and
I may not see the errors of the hour totter to their
fall, but I shall be perfectly content to sleep in Christ,
for I have a sure expectation that this work will suc-
ceed in the end. I shall be happy to have done my
share of the work, even if I personally see little ap-
parent result. Lord, let Thy work appear unto Thy
servants, and we will be content that Thy glory should
be reserved for our children. Stand fast, my brethren,
in incessant labors, for the end is sure.

And then, in addition to standing fast in that respect,
stand fast *without warping*. Timber, when it is rather
green, is apt to go this way or that. The spiritual
weather is very bad just now for green wood: it is one
day damp with superstition, and another day it is
parched with skepticism. Rationalism and Ritualism are
both at work. I pray that you may not warp. Keep
straight; keep to the truth, the whole truth, and nothing
but the truth; for in the Master's name we bid you
"Stand fast in the Lord."

Stand fast, for there is great need. Many walk of whom I have told you often, and now tell you even weeping, that they are the enemies of the cross of Christ.

III. Thirdly, THE APOSTLE URGED THE BEST MOTIVES FOR THEIR STANDING FAST.

He says, "Stand fast *because of your citizenship.*" Read the twentieth verse; "For our citizenship is in heaven." Now, if you are what you profess to be, if you are in Christ, you are citizens of the New Jerusalem. Men ought to behave themselves according to their citizenship, and not dishonor their city.

When a man was a citizen of Athens, in the olden time, he felt it incumbent upon him to be brave. Xerxes said, "These Athenians are not ruled by kings: how will they fight?" "No," said one, "but every man respects the law, and each man is ready to die for his country." Xerxes soon had to know that the like obedience and respect of law ruled the Spartans, and that these, because they were of Sparta, were all brave as lions. He sends word to Leonidas and his little troop to give up their arms. "Come and take them," was the courageous reply. The Persian king had myriads of soldiers with him, while Leonidas had only three hundred Spartans at his side; yet they kept the pass, and it cost the eastern despot many thousands of men to force a passage. The sons of Sparta died rather than desert their post. Every citizen of Sparta felt that he must stand fast: it was not for such a man as he to yield.

I like the spirit of Bayard, that "knight without fear and without reproach." He knew not what fear meant. In his last battle, his spine was broken, and he said

to those around him, "Place me up against a tree, so
that I may sit up and die with my face to the enemy."
Yes, if our backs were broken, if we could no more
bear the shield or use the sword, it would be incumbent
upon us, as citizens of the New Jerusalem, to die with
our faces towards the enemy.

We must not yield, we dare not yield, if we are of
the city of the great King. The martyrs cry to us to
stand fast; the cloud of witnesses bending from their
thrones above beseech us to stand fast; yea, all the
hosts of the shining ones cry to us "Stand fast." Stand
fast for God, and the truth, and holiness, and let no
man take your crown.

The next argument that Paul used was *their outlook*.
"Our conversation is in heaven; from whence also we
look for the Saviour, the Lord Jesus Christ." Brethren,
Jesus is coming. He is even now on the way. You
have heard our tidings till you scarcely credit us; but
the word is true, and it will surely be fulfilled before
long. The Lord is coming indeed. He promised to
come to die, and He kept His word: He now promises
to come to reign, and be you sure that He will keep
His tryst with His people. He is coming. Ears of faith
can hear the sound of His chariot wheels; every moment of time, every event of providence is bringing
Him nearer. Blessed are those servants who shall not
be sleeping when He comes, nor wandering from their
posts of duty; happy shall they be whom their Lord
shall find faithfully watching, and standing fast in that
great day!

To us, beloved, He is coming, not as Judge and De-
stroyer, but as *Saviour*. We look for the Saviour, the
Lord Jesus Christ. Now, if we look for Him, let us

"stand fast." There must be no going into sin, no
forsaking the fellowship of the church, no leaving the
truth, no trying to play fast and loose with godliness,
no running with the hare and hunting with the hounds.
Let us stand so fast in singleness of heart that, whenever Jesus comes, we shall be able to say, "Welcome,
welcome, Son of God!"

Sometimes I wait through the weary years with great
comfort. There was a ship some time ago outside a
certain harbor. A heavy sea made the ship roll fearfully.
A dense fog blotted out all buoys and lights. The
captain never left the wheel. He could not tell his
way into the harbor, and no pilot could get out to him
for a long time. Eager passengers urged him to be
courageous and make a dash for the harbor. He said
"No; it is not my duty to run so great a risk. A pilot
is required here, and I will wait for one if I wait a
week."

The truest courage is that which can bear to be
charged with cowardice. To wait is much wiser than
when you cannot hear the fog-horn and have no pilot
yet to steam on and wreck your vessel on the rocks.
Our prudent captain waited his time, and at last he
espied the pilot's boat coming to him over the boiling
sea. When the pilot was at his work the captain's
anxious waiting was over.

The Church is like the vessel, she is pitched to and
fro in the storm and the dark, and the Pilot has not
yet come. The weather is very threatening. All around
the darkness hangs like a pall. But Jesus will come,
walking on the water, before long; He will bring us
safe to the desired haven. Let us wait with patience.

Stand fast! Stand fast! for Jesus is coming, and in Him is our sure hope.

Further, there was another motive. *There was an expectation.* "He shall change our vile body," or rather, "body of our humiliation." Only think of it, dear friends! No more headaches or heartaches, no more feebleness and fainting, no more inward tumor or consumption; but the Lord shall transfigure this body of our humiliation into the likeness of the body of His glory. Our frame is now made up of decaying substances, it is of the earth earthy. "So to the dust return we must." This body groans, suffers, becomes diseased, and dies: blessed be God, it shall be wonderfully changed, and then there shall be no more death, neither sorrow nor crying, neither shall there be any more pain.

The natural appetites of this body engender sad tendencies to sin, and in this respect it is a "vile body." It shall not always be so! the great change will deliver it from all that is gross and carnal. It shall be pure as the Lord's body! Whatever the body of Christ is now, our body is to be like it. We are to have a real, corporeal body as He had for substance and reality; and, like His body, it will be full of beauty, full of health and strength; it will enjoy peculiar immunities from evil, and special adaptations for good.

That is what is going to happen to me and to you · therefore let us stand fast. Let us not wilfully throw away our prospects of glory and immortality. What! Relinquish resurrection? Relinquish glory? Relinquish likeness to the risen Lord? O God, save us from such a terrible piece of apostasy! Save us from such immeasurable folly! Suffer us not to turn our backs in the day of battle, since that would be to turn our backs from the crown of life that fadeth not away.

Lastly, the apostle urges us to stand fast because of *our resources*. Somebody may ask, "How can this body of ours be transformed and transfigured until it becomes like the body of Christ?" I cannot tell you anything about the process; it will all be accomplished in the twinkling of an eye, at the last trump. But I can tell you by what power it will be accomplished. The Omnipotent Lord will lay bare His arm, and exercise His might, "according to the working whereby he is able even to subdue all things unto himself."

O brethren, we may well stand fast since we have infinite power at our backs. The Lord is with us with all His energy, even with His all-conquering strength, which shall yet subdue all His foes. Do not let us imagine that any enemy can be too strong for Christ's arm. If He is able to subdue all things unto Himself, He can certainly bear us through all opposition. One glance of His eye may wither all opposers, or, better still, one word from His lips may turn them into friends.

The army of the Lord is strong in reserves. These reserves have never yet been fully called out. We, who are in the field, are only a small squadron, holding the fort; but our Lord has at His back ten thousand times ten thousand who will carry war into the enemy's camp. When the Captain of our salvation comes to the front, He will bring His heavenly legions with Him. Our business is to watch until He appears upon the scene, for when He comes, His infinite resources will be put in marching order.

I like that speech of Wellington (who was so calm amid the roar of Waterloo), when an officer sent word,

"Tell the Commander-in-Chief that he must move me,
I cannot hold my position any longer, my numbers are
so thinned." "Tell him," said the great general, "He
must hold his place. Every Englishman today must die
where he stands, or else win the victory." The officer
read the command to stand, and he did stand till the
trumpet sounded victory.

And so it is now. My brethren, we must die where
we are rather than yield to the enemy. If Jesus tarries
we must not desert our posts. Wellington knew that
the heads of the Prussian columns would soon be visible,
coming in to ensure the victory; and so by faith we
can perceive the legions of our Lord approaching: in
serried ranks His angels fly through the opening heaven.
The air is teeming with them. I hear their silver trum-
pets. Behold, He cometh with clouds! When He cometh He will abundantly recompense all who stood fast
amid the rage of battle. Let us sing, "Hold the fort,
for I am coming."

CHAPTER III

NEVERTHELESS, HEREAFTER

"Jesus saith unto him, Thou hast said (or said so), nevertheless, I say unto you, Hereafter shall ye see the Son of man sitting on the right hand of power, and coming in the clouds of heaven" (Matthew 26:64).

OUR LORD, before His enemies, was silent in His own defense, but He faithfully warned and boldly avowed the truth. His was the silence of patience, not of indifference; of courage, not of cowardice. It is written that "before Pontius Pilate He witnessed a good confession," and that statement may also be well applied to His utterances before Caiaphas, for there He was not silent when it came to confession of necessary truth.

If you will read the chapter now open before us, you will notice that the high priest adjured Him, saying, "Art thou the Christ, the Son of God?" to which He replied at once, "Thou hast said it." He did not disown His Messiahship; He claimed to be the promised one, the messenger from heaven, Christ the anointed of the Most High. Neither did He for a moment disavow His personal deity: He acknowledged and confessed that He was the Son of God. How could He be silent when such a vital point as to His person was in question? He did not hold them in suspense, but openly declared His Godhead by saying, "I am"; for so are His words reported by one of the evangelists. He

49

then proceeded to reveal the solemn fact that He would soon sit at the right hand of God, even the Father.

In the words of our next text He declared that those who were condemning Him would see Him glorified, and in due time would stand at His bar when He would come upon the clouds of heaven to judge the quick and dead according to our gospel. See, then, dear brethren, in a few words, the great truths of our holy religion clearly set forth by our Lord Jesus: He claimed to be the Christ of God, and the Son of God, and His brief statement by implication speaks of Jesus dead, buried, and risen, and now enthroned at the right hand of God in the power of the Father, and Jesus soon to come in His glorious second advent to judge the world in righteousness. Our Lord's confession was very full, and happy is he who heartily embraces it.

I intend to dwell upon three catch-words around which there gathers a world of encouraging and solemn thought. The first is *"nevertheless,"* and the second is *"hereafter"*; what the third is you shall know hereafter, but not just now.

I. "NEVERTHELESS," said Christ, "hereafter shall ye see the Son of man sitting at the right hand of power, and coming in the clouds of heaven." This, then, is the string from which we must draw forth music. *"Nevertheless,"* which being interpreted by being pulled in pieces, signifies that truth is never-the-less sure because of opposition. "Nevertheless," not one atom the less is the truth certain to prevail, for all that you say or do against it. Jesus will surely sit at the right hand of power, and come in due season upon the clouds of heaven. Let us dwell for a little time upon this important fact, that truth is none the less certain because of the opposition of men and devils.

Observe, first, that *the Saviour's condition when He made use of that "nevertheless" was no proof that He would not rise to power.* There He stood, a poor, defenseless, emaciated Man, newly led from the night-watch in the garden and its bloody sweat. *He was a spectacle of meek and lowly suffering,* led by His captors like a lamb to the slaughter, with none to speak a word on His behalf. He was surrounded by those who hated Him, and He was forsaken by His friends. Scribes, Pharisees, priests, were all thirsting for His heart's blood.

A lamb in the midst of wolves is but a faint picture of Christ standing there before the Sanhedrim in patient silence. And yet, though His present condition seemed to contradict it, He who was the faithful and true witness spake truly when He testified, "Nevertheless, hereafter ye shall see the Son of man coming in the clouds of heaven. Despite My present shame and suffering, so it shall be."

He gives Himself that humble title of Son of man, as best indicating Himself in His condition at that time. "Hereafter ye shall see the Son of man sitting at the right hand of power, and coming in the clouds of heaven." The humiliation of Christ did not in the least endanger His after glory. His sufferings, His shame, His death, did not render it any the less certain that He would climb to His throne. Nor did the cavillings of His opposers keep Him for one instant from His place of honor. I wish you to remember this, for there is a great principle in it.

There are many poor weakminded people who cannot take sides with a persecuted truth, nor accept anything but the most popular and fashionable form of religion. They dare not be with truth when men spit in its face, and buffet it, and pour contempt upon it; but it will be victorious none the less, although cowards desert it and falsehearted men oppose it. If it stand alone at the bar of the world, a culprit to be condemned, if it receive nothing but a universal hiss of human execration—yet, if it be the truth, it may be condemned, but it will be justified; it may be buried, but it will rise; it may be rejected, but it will be glorified, even as it has happened to the Christ of God.

Who would be ashamed of truth at any time when he knows the preciousness of it? Who will tremble because of present opposition when he foresees what will yet come of it? What a sublime spectacle—the Man of sorrows standing before His cruel judges in all manner of weakness and poverty and contempt, at the same time heir of all things, and appointed, nevertheless, to sit at the right hand of power and to come in the clouds of heaven.

Nor may we think only of His condition as a despised and rejected man; for He was, on His trial, charged with grievous wrong, and about to be *condemned by the ecclesiastical authorities*. The scribes learned in the law declared that He blasphemed: and the priests, familiar with the ordinances of God, exclaimed, "Away with Him; it is not meet that He should live." The high priest himself gave judgment that it was expedient for Him to be put to death.

It is a very serious thing, is it not, when all the ecclesiastical authorities are against you—when they are unanimous in your condemnation? Yes, verily, and it may cause great searching of heart; for no peaceable man desires to be opposed to constituted authority, but would sooner have the good word of those who sit in Moses' seat. But this was not the last time in which the established ecclesiastical authorities were wrong, grievously wrong. They were condemning the innocent, and blaspheming the Lord from heaven. Nor, I say, was this the last time in which the mitre and the gown have been upon the side of cruel wrong: yet this did not un-Christ our Saviour or rob Him of His deity or His throne.

On the same principle human history brings before us abundance of instances in which, nevertheless, though scribes, priests, bishops, pontiffs, and popes condemned the truth, it was just as sure, and became as triumphant, as it had a right to do. There stands the one lone Man, and there are all the great ones around Him— men of authority and reputation, sanctity and pomp— and they unanimously deny that He can ever sit at the right hand of God: "But, nevertheless," saith He, "here- after ye shall see the Son of man at the right hand of power." He spoke the truth: His declaration has been most gloriously fulfilled hitherto. Even thus over the neck of clergy, priests, pontiffs, popes, His triumphant chariot of salvation shall still roll, and the truth—the simple truth of His glorious gospel—shall, despite them all, win the day, and reign over the sons of men.

Nor is this all. Our Lord at that time was *surrounded by those who were in possession of earthly power.* The priests had the ear of Pilate, and Pilate had the Roman legions at his back. Who could resist such a combina- tion of force? Craft and authority form a dreadful league. One disciple drew a sword, but just at the

time when our Lord stood before the Sanhedrim that
one chivalrous warrior had denied him; so that all the
physical force was on the other side. As a man He was
helpless when He stood bound before the council. I am
not speaking now of that almighty power which faith
knows to have dwelt in Him; but as to human power
He was weakness at its weakest. His cause seemed
at the lowest ebb. He had none to stand up in His
defense—nay, none to speak a word on His behalf;
for, "Who shall declare his generation?"

And yet, for all that, and even because of it, He did
rise to sit at the right hand of power, and He shall come
in the clouds of heaven. So if it ever comes to pass, my
brother, that thou shouldst be the lone advocate of a
forgotten truth—if thy Master should ever put thee in
all thy weakness and infirmity in the midst of the mighty
and the strong, do not thou fear or tremble; for the
possession of power is but a trifle compared with the
possession of truth, and he that has the right may
safely defy the might of the world. He shall win and
conquer, let the princes and powers that be take to themselves what force and craft they choose. Jesus, nevertheless, wins, though the power is all against Him, and
so shall the truth which He represents, for it wears
about it a hidden power which baffles all opponents.

Nor was it merely all the power, there was *a great
deal of furious rage against Him.* That Caiaphas, how
he spoke to Him! "I adjure thee," saith he, "by God."
And after he has spoken he rends his garments in in-
dignation, his anger burns like fire; but the Christ is
very quiet, the Lamb of God is still, and looking His
adversary in the face, He says, "Nevertheless, hereafter
thou shalt see the Son of man sitting at the right hand

of power, and coming in the clouds of heaven." He was strong, and therefore calm; confident, and therefore peaceful; fully assured, and therefore patient. He could wait, for He believed; and His prophecy was true, notwithstanding the high priest's rage. So if we meet with any man at any time who gnashes his teeth upon us, who foams in passion, who dips his pen in the bitterest gall to write down our holy faith, who is indefatigable in his violent efforts against the Christ of God—what mattereth it? "Nevertheless, ye shall see the Son of man sitting at the right hand of power." "Yet have I set my king upon my holy hill of Zion," said Jehovah; and He declared the decree though the heathen raged and the people imagined a vain thing. Well may he smile at rage who is sure of victory.

Yes, but it was not one person that raged merely. The people of Jerusalem, and the multitudes that had come up to the passover, bribed and egged on by the priests and the Pharisees, were all hot after our Saviour's death, clamoring, "Crucify him, Crucify him"; and yet there He stood, and as He heard their tumult, and anticipated its growing demand for His blood, He lost not His confidence, but He calmly said, "Nevertheless, hereafter, shall ye see the Son of man sitting at the right hand of power."

Beloved, you know that after He had said this our Lord was taken before Herod and Pilate, and at last was put to death: and He knew all this, foreseeing it most clearly, and yet it did not make Him hesitate. He knew that He would be crucified, and that His enemies would boast that there was an end of Him and of His kingdom. He knew that His disciples would hide themselves in holes and corners, and that nobody would

dare to say a word concerning the man of Nazareth: He
foreknew that the name of the Nazarene would be
bandied about amid general opprobrium, and Jerusalem
would say, "That cause is crushed out: that egg of mis-
chief has been broken"; but He, foreseeing all that,
and more, declared, "Nevertheless, hereafter ye shall see
the Son of man sitting at the right hand of power, and
coming in the clouds of heaven."

I cannot help harping upon the text—I hope I shall
not weary you with it, for to me it is music. I do not
like running over the word *"nevertheless"* too quickly,
I like to draw it out and repeat it as "never—the—less."
No, not one jot the less will His victory come. Not
in the least degree was His royal power endangered or
His sure triumph imperilled. Not even by His death
and the consequent scattering of His disciples was the
least hazard occasioned; but, indeed, all these things
wrought together for the accomplishment of the divine
purpose concerning Him, and the lower He stooped
the more sure He was to rise ultimately to His glory.

Before long He will come. We cannot tell when:
He may come tonight, or He may tarry many a weary
year: but He will surely come in person, for did not
the angels say to the men of Galilee, as they stood
gazing into heaven, "This same Jesus shall so come in
like manner as ye have seen him go into heaven"? He
shall come with blast of trumpet and with thousands
of angelic beings, all doing Him honor. He shall come
with flaming fire to visit the trembling earth. He shall
come with all His Father's glories on, and kings and
princes shall stand before Him, and He shall reign
amongst His ancients gloriously. The tumults of the
people, and the plottings of their ruler, shall be remem-

bered in that day, but it shall be to their own eternal
shame: His throne shall be none the less resplendent.

I beg you to learn the spiritual lesson which comes
out of this. I have already indicated it, and it is this—
never be afraid to stand by a losing cause. Never hesitate to stand alone when the truth is to be confessed.
Never be overawed by sacerdotalism, or daunted by
rage, or swayed by multitudes. Unpopular truth is,
nevertheless, eternal, and that doctrine which is scouted
and cast out as evil today shall bring immortal honor
to the man who dares to stand by its side and share
its humiliation.

Oh, for the love of the Christ who thus threw a
"nevertheless" at the feet of His foes, follow Him
whithersoever He goeth. Through flood or flame, in
loneliness, in shame, in obloquy, in reproach, follow
Him! If it be without the camp, follow Him! If every
step shall cost you abuse and scorn, follow still; yea,
to prison and to death still follow Him, for as surely
as He sitteth at the right hand of power so shall those
who love Him and have been faithful to His truth sit
down upon His throne with Him. His overcoming and
enthronement are the pledges of the victory both of the
truth and of those who courageously espouse it.

Thus have we sounded our first great bell—"NEVER-
THELESS." Let its music ring through the place and
charm each opened ear.

II. The second bell is "HEREAFTER." "Nevertheless,
hereafter." I like the sound of those two bells together:
let us ring them again. "Nevertheless, *hereafter.*" The
hereafter seems in brief to say to me that *the main glory
of Christ lies in the future.* Not today, perhaps, nor tomorrow will the issue be seen! Have patience! Wait a

while, "Your strength is to sit still." God has great leisure, for He is the Eternal. Let us partake in His restfulness while we sing, *"Nevertheless, hereafter."* O for the Holy Spirit's power at this moment; for it is written, "He will show you things to come."

It is one great reason why the unregenerate sons of men cannot see any glory in the kingdom of Christ because to them it is such a future thing. Its hopes look into eternity: its great rewards are beyond this present time and state, and the most of mortal eyes cannot see so far. Unregenerate men are like Passion in John Bunyan's parable: they will have all their good things now, and so they have their toys and break them, and they are gone, and then their hereafter is a dreary outlook of regret and woe.

Men of faith know better; and like Patience in the same parable, they choose to have their best things last, for that which comes last, lasts on for ever. He whose turn comes last has none to follow him, and his good things shall never be taken away from him. The poor, purblind world cannot see beyond its own nose, and so it must have its joys and riches at once. To them speedy victory is the main thing, and the truth is nothing. Is the cause triumphant today? Off with your caps, and throw them up, and cry "Hurrah!" no matter that it is the cause of a lie. Do the multitudes incline that way? Then, sir, if you be worldly-wise, run with them. Pull off the palm branches, strew the roads, and shout "Hosanna to the hero of the hour!" though he be a despot or a deceiver.

But not so—not so with those who are taught of God. They take eternity into their estimate, and they are contented to go with the despised and rejected of men for the present, because they recollect the hereafter. They can swim against the flood, for they know whither the course of this world is tending. O blind world, if thou wert wise, thou wouldst amend thy line of action, and begin to think of the hereafter too; for, brethren, the hereafter will soon be *here*. What a short time it is since Adam walked in the garden of Eden: compared with the ages of the rocks, compared with the history of the stars, compared with the life of God, it is as the winking of an eye, or as a flash of lightning. One has but to grow a little older, and years become shorter, and time appears to travel at a much faster rate than before, so that a year rushes by you like a meteor across the midnight heavens.

When we are older still, and look down from the serene abodes above, I suppose that centuries and ages will be as moments to us; for to the Lord they are as nothing. Suppose the coming of the Lord should be put off for ten thousand years—it is but supposition—but if it were, ten thousand years will soon be gone, and when the august spectacle of Christ coming on the clouds of heaven shall really be seen, the delay will be as though but an hour had intervened. The space between now and then, or rather the space between what is "now" at this time, and what will be "now" at the last—how short a span it is! Men will look back from the eternal world and say, "How could we have thought so much of the fleeting life we have lived on earth, when it was to be followed by eternity? What fools we were to make such count of momentary, transient pleasures, when now the things which are not seen, and are eternal, have come upon us, and we are unprepared for them!"

Christ will soon come, and at the longest, when He cometh, the interval between today and then will seem to be just nothing at all; so that "hereafter" is not as the sound of far-off cannon, nor as the boom of distant thunder, but it is the rolling of rushing wheels hastening to overtake us.

"Hereafter!" "Hereafter!" Oh, when that hereafter comes, how overwhelming it will be to Jesus' foes! Now where is Caiaphas? Will he now adjure the Lord to speak? Now, ye priests, lift up your haughty heads! Utter a sentence against Him now! There sits your victim upon the clouds of heaven. Say now that He blasphemes, and hold up your rent rags, and condemn Him again.

But where is Caiaphas? He hides his guilty head: he is utterly confounded, and begs the mountains to fall upon him. And, oh, ye men of the Sanhedrim, who sat at midnight and glared on your innocent victim, with your cold, cruel eyes, and afterwards gloated over the death of your martyred Prince, where are ye now— now that He has come with all His Father's power to judge you? They are asking the hills to open their caverns and conceal them: the rocks deny them shelter. And where, on that day, will you be; you who deny His deity, who profane His Sabbath, who slander His people, and denounce His gospel—oh, where will you be in that tremendous day, which as surely comes as comes tomorrow's rising sun?

Oh, sirs, consider this word—"Hereafter!" I would fain whisper it in the ear of the sinner, fascinated by his pleasures. Come near and let me do so—*hereafter!* I would make it the alarum of the bed-head of the sleeping transgressor, who is dreaming of peace and safety, while he is slumbering himself into hell. Hereafter! Hereafter! Oh, yes, ye may suck the sweet, and eat the fat, and drink as ye will; but hereafter! hereafter! What will ye do hereafter when that which is sweet in the mouth shall be as gall in the belly, and when the pleasures of today shall be a mixture of misery for eternity? Hereafter! Oh, hereafter! Now, O Spirit divine, be pleased to open careless ears, that they may listen to this prophetic sound.

To the Lord's own people there is no sound more sweet than that of "hereafter." "Hereafter ye shall see the Son of man coming in the clouds of heaven." Welcome, welcome, welcome, welcome, Redeemer, Saviour! Welcome in every character in which Thou comest. What acclamations and congratulations will go up from the countless myriads of His redeemed, when first the ensigns of the Son of man shall be seen in the heavens!

On some one of earth's mornings, when the children of men shall be "marrying and giving in marriage," while saints shall be looking for His appearing, they shall first of all perceive that He is actually coming. Long desired, and come at last. Then the trumpet shall be heard, waxing exceeding loud and long, ringing out a sweeter note to the true Israel than ever trumpet heard on the morn of Jubilee.

What delight! What lifting up of gladsome eyes! What floods of bliss! Oppression is over, the idols are broken, the reign of sin is ended, darkness shall no more cover the nations. He cometh, He cometh: glory be to His name!

> "Bring forth the royal diadem,
> And crown Him Lord of all."

O blessed day of acclamations! how shall heaven's vault be rent with them when His saints shall see for them-

selves what was reserved for Him and for them in
the "hereafter." "Ye shall see the Son of man at the
right hand of power, and coming in the clouds of
heaven."

That word "hereafter," my brothers and sisters,
is, at this moment, our grandest solace, and I wish
to bring it before you in that light. Have you been
misunderstood, misrepresented, slandered because of
fidelity to the right and to the true? Do not trouble
yourself. Vindicate not your own cause. Refer it to
the King's Bench above, and say, "Hereafter, hereafter."

Have you been accused of being mad, fanatical, and
I know not what besides, because to you party is nothing, and ecclesiastical pride nothing, and the stamp of
popular opinion nothing; because you are determined
to follow the steps of your Master, and believe the true
and do the right? Then be in no hurry; the sure hereafter will settle the debate. Or are you very poor, and
very sick, and very sad? But are you Christ's own? Do
you trust Him? Do you live in fellowship with Him?
Then the hope of the hereafter may well take the sting
out of the present.

It is not for long that you shall suffer; the glory will
soon be revealed in you and around you. There are
streets of gold symbolic of your future wealth, and there
are harps celestial emblematical of your eternal joy.
You shall have a white robe soon, and the dusty garments of toil shall be laid aside for ever. You shall
have a far more exceeding and an eternal weight of
glory; and therefore the light affliction which is but
for a moment may well be endured with patience.

Have you labored in vain? Have you tried to bring
souls to Christ, and had no recompense? Fret not, but

remember the hereafter. Many a laborer, unsuccessful
to the eye of man, will receive a "Well done, good
and faithful servant" from his Master in that day.
Set little store by anything you have, and wish but
lightly for anything that you have not. Let the present
be to you, as it really is, a dream, an empty show, and
project your soul into the hereafter, which is solid and
enduring; for, oh! what music there is in it!—what delight to a true child of God! "Nevertheless, hereafter."

I feel half inclined to have done, and to send you
out of the place, singing all the way, "Nevertheless,
hereafter." The people outside might not understand
you, but it would be a perfectly justifiable enthusiasm
of delight.

III. Now, thirdly. Where am I to look for my third
bell? Where is the third word I spoke of? In truth,
I cannot find it in the version which we commonly use,
and there is no third word in the original, and yet the
word I am thinking of is there. The truth is that the
second word, which has been rendered by "hereafter,"
bears another meaning; I will give you what the Greek
critics say, as nearly as can be, the meaning of the word
is, "HENCEFORWARD." "Henceforward ye shall see the
Son of man sitting at the right hand of power, and
coming in the clouds of heaven."

"*Henceforward.*" That is another word and the
teaching gathered out of it is this: *even in the present
there are tokens of the victory of Christ.* "But," says
one, "did Christ say to those priests that henceforward
they should see Him sitting at the right hand of power?
Yes, yes, that is what He meant. He meant, "You look
at Me and scorn Me; but, sirs, you shall not be able
to do this any longer, for henceforward you shall see

for yourselves that I am not what I appear to be, but that I sit at the right hand of power. Henceforward, and as long as you live, you shall know that galling truth."

And did that come true? Yes, it came true that night; for when the Saviour died there came a messenger unto the members of the Sanhedrim and others, and told them that the veil of the temple was rent in twain. In that moment, when the Man of Nazareth died, that splendid piece of tapestry seemed to tear itself asunder from end to end as if in horror at the death of its Lord. The members of that council, when they met each other in the street and spoke of the news, must have been dumb in sheer astonishment; but while they looked upon each other the earth they stood upon reeled and reeled again, and they could scarcely keep their feet. This was not the first wonder which had that day startled them, for the sun had been beclouded in unnatural darkness. At midday the sun had ceased to shine, and now the earth ceases to be stable.

Lo, also, in the darkness of the evening, certain members of this council saw the sheeted dead, newly arisen from their sepulchres, walking through the streets; for the rocks rent, the earth shook, and the graves opened, and the dead came forth and appeared unto many. Thus early they began to know that the Man of Nazareth was at the right hand of power.

Early on the third morning, when they were met together, there came a messenger in hot haste, who said, "The stone is rolled away from the door of the sepulchre. Remember that ye placed a watch, and that ye set your seal upon the stone. But early this morning the soldiers say that He came forth. He rose, that dreaded

One whom we put to death, and at the sight of Him the keepers did quake and became as dead men."

Now, these men—these members of the Sanhedrim—believed that fact; and we have clear evidence that they did so, for they bribed the soldiers, and said, "Say ye, his disciples came and stole away his body while we slept." Then did the word also continue to be fulfilled, and they plainly saw that Jesus whom they had condemned was at the right hand of power. A few weeks passed over their heads, and, lo, there was a noise in the city, and an extraordinary excitement. Peter had been preaching and three thousand persons in one day had been baptized into the name which they dreaded so much; and they were told, and they heard it on the best of evidence, that there had been a wonderful manifestation of the Holy Spirit, such as was spoken of in the book of the prophet Joel.

Then they must have looked one another in the face, and stroked their beards, and bitten their lips, and said one to another, "Did he not say that we should see him at the right hand of power?" They had often to remember that word, and again and again to see its truth, for when Peter and John were brought before them, it was proven that they had restored a lame man, and these two unlearned and ignorant men told them that it was through the name of Jesus that the lame were made to leap and walk.

Day after day they were continuously obliged, against their will, to see, in the spread of the religion of the Man whom they had put to death, that His name had power about it such as they could not possibly gainsay or resist. Lo, one of their number, Paul, had been converted, and was preaching the faith which he had endeavored to destroy. They must have been much amazed and chagrined, as in this also they discerned that the Son of man was at the right hand of power.

Read the text as meaning, "Henceforward, ye shall see the Son of man at the right hand of power, and coming in the clouds of heaven." It is not the full meaning of the passage, but it is a part of that meaning, beyond all question.

Beloved, even at the present time we may see the tokens of the power of Christ among us. Only tokens, mark you; I do not want to take you off from the hereafter, but henceforward and even now there are tokens of the power of our Lord Jesus. Look at revivals. When they break out in the church how they stagger all the adversaries of Christ. They said—yes, they dared to say —that the gospel had lost all its power—that, since the days of Whitefield and Wesley, there was no hope of the masses being stirred, yet when they see, even in this house, from Sabbath to Sabbath, vast crowds listening to the word, and when some few months ago no house could be built that was large enough to accommodate the thronging masses who sought to hear our American brethren, then were they smitten in the mouth, so that they could speak no more, for it was manifested that the Lord Christ still lives, and that, if His gospel be fully and simply preached, it will still draw all men to Him, and the souls will be saved, and that not a few.

And look ye, in the brave world outside, apart from religion, what influences there are abroad which are due to the power of the Christ of God. Would you have believed it twenty years ago that in America there should be no more a slave; that united Italy should be free of her despots? Could you have believed that the Pope would be puling about his being a prisoner in the Vatican, and that the power of anti-Christ would be shorn away? No, the wonders of history, even within the last few years, are enough to show us that Christ is at the right hand of power. Come what will in the future, mark ye this, my brethren, it will never be possible to uphold tyranny and oppression long, for the Lord Christ is to the front for the poor and needy of the earth.

O despots, you may do what you will, and use your craft and policy, if you please, but all over this world the Lord Jesus Christ has lifted up a plummet and set up a righteous standard, and He will draw a straight line, and it will pass through everything that offends, that it may be cut off; and it will also pass over all that is good and lovely, and right, and just, and true, and these shall be established in His reign among men. I believe in the reign of Christ. Kings, sultans, czars— these are puppets all of them, and your parliaments and congresses are but vanity of vanity. God is great, and none but He. Jesus is the King in all the earth. He is the Man, the King of men, the Lord of all. Glory be to His name.

As the years progress we shall see it more and more, for He has had long patience, but He is beginning now to cut the work short in righteousness. He is baring His right arm for war and that which denies manhood's just claims, that which treads upon the neck of the humanity which Christ has taken, that which stands against His throne and dominion, must be broken in pieces like a potter's vessel, for the scepter in His hand is a rod of iron, and He will use it mightily. The

Christ, then, gives tokens still of His power. They are only tokens, but they are sure ones, even as the dawn does not deceive us, though it be not the noontide.

And oh, let me say, there be some of you present who are enemies of Christ, but you also must have perceived some tokens of His power. I have seen Him shake the infidel by the gospel till He has said, "Almost thou persuadest me to be a Christian." He has taken him in the silence of the night and probed his conscience: in His gentleness and love, and pity He has led the man to think, and though he has not altogether yielded, yet he has felt that there is a solemn power about the Christ of God. Some of the worst of men have been forced to own that Christ has conquered them.

Remember how Julian, as he died, said, "The Nazarene has overcome me: the Nazarene has overcome me." May you not have to say that in the article of death, but oh that you may say it now. May His love overpower you, may His compassion win you, and you will see in your own salvation tokens of His power.

But I must have done, for my time has fled, but I desire to add that it will be a blessed thing if everyone here, becoming a believer in Jesus, shall henceforward see Him at the right hand of power and coming in the clouds of heaven. Would to God we could live with that vision full in view, believing Jesus to be at the right hand of power, trusting Him and resting in Him. Because we know Him to be the Lord, strong and mighty, the Lord mighty in battle, we ought never to have a doubt when we are doing what is right. We ought never to have a doubt when we are following

Jesus, for He is more than a conqueror, and so shall His followers be. Let us go on courageously, trusting in Him as a child trusts in his father, for He is mighty upon whom we repose our confidence.

Let us also keep before our mind's eye the fact that He is coming. Be ye not as the virgins that fell asleep. Even now my ear seems to hear the midnight cry, "Behold, the bridegroom cometh!" Arise, ye virgins, sleep no longer, for the bridegroom is near.

As for you, ye foolish virgins, God grant that there may yet be time enough left to awake even you, that you may yet have oil for your lamps before He comes. He comes we know not when, but He comes quickly. Be ye ready, for in such an hour as ye think not the Son of man cometh. Be ye as men that watch for their Lord, and as servants that are ready to give in their account, because the master of the house is near.

In that spirit let us come to the Lord's table, as often as we gather there, for He has said to us, "Do this until I come." Outward ordinances will cease when He comes, for we shall need no memorial when the Lord Himself will be among us. Let us here pledge Him in the cup. That He is coming we do verily believe; that He is coming we do joyfully proclaim. Is it a subject of joy to you? If not—

> "Ye sinners seek His face,
>   Whose wrath ye cannot bear;
>   Bow to the scepter of His grace,
>   And find salvation there."

God bless you for Christ's sake.

CHAPTER IV

COME, MY BELOVED

"Make haste, my beloved, and be thou like to a roe or to a young hart upon the mountains of spices" (Solomon's Song 8:14).

THE SONG OF SONGS describes the love of Jesus Christ to His people, and it ends with an intense desire on the part of the Church that the Lord Jesus should come back to her. The last word of the lover to the Beloved One is, "Speed thy return; make haste and come back."

Is it not somewhat singular that, as the last verse of the Book of love has this note in it, so the last verses of the whole Book of God, which I may also call the Book of love, have that same thought in them? At the twentieth verse of the last chapter of the Revelation, we read, "He which testifieth these things saith, Surely I come quickly. Amen. Even so, come, Lord Jesus." The Song of love and the Book of love end in almost the selfsame way, with a strong desire for Christ's speedy return.

Are your hearts, dear friends, in tune with that desire? They ought to be, yet have not some of you almost forgotten that Jesus is to come a second time? Refresh your memories. Others of you, who know that He will come, have you not thought of it as a doctrine that might be laid by on the shelf? Have you not been without any desire for His glorious appearing? Is this right? That Song of Solomon is the central Book of the Bible; it is the innermost shrine of divine revelation, the holy of holies of Scripture; and if you are living in communion with God, you will love that Book, you will catch its spirit, and you will be inclined to cry with the spouse, "Make haste, my beloved."

If you have no longings for Christ's appearance, no desires for His speedy return, surely your heart is sick, and your love is faint. I fear that you are getting into a lukewarm state. I believe that our relationship to the Second Advent of Christ may be used as a thermometer with which to tell the degree of our spiritual heat. If we have strong desires, longing desires, burning desires, for the coming of the Lord, we may hope that it is well with us; but if we have no such desires, I think, at best, we must be somewhat careless; perhaps, to take the worst view of our case, we are sadly declining in grace.

I. Well now, to come to our text; I want you to notice, first, WHAT THE CHURCH CALLS HER LORD: "Make haste, *my Beloved.*"

I will have only a few words upon this point. I am hardly going to preach tonight, but just to talk familiarly to you, and I want you to let your hearts talk. Observe, the spouse first calls her Lord, "Beloved," and secondly, "My Beloved."

Christ is our *"Beloved."* This is a word of affection; and our Lord Jesus Christ is the object of affection to us. If you read the Bible, especially if you read the New Testament, and study the life of Christ, and yet you only admire it, and say to yourself, "Jesus Christ was a wonderful being," you do not know Him yet; you have but a very indistinct idea of Him.

If, after reading that life, you sit down, and dissect it, and say to yourself, coolly, calmly, deliberately, "So far as is practicable, I will try and imitate Christ," you do not yet know Him, you have not come near to the real Christ as yet. If any man should say, "I am near the fire," and yet he is not warm, I should question the truth of his words; and though he might say, "I can see the fire; I can tell you the appearance of the coals; I can describe the lambent flames that play about the stove," yet if he were not warmed at all, I should still think that he was mistaken, or that there was some medium that interposed between him and the fire at which he said he was looking.

But when you really come to see Jesus, and to say, "I love Him; my heart yearns toward Him; my delight is in Him; He has won my love, and holds it in His own heart," then you begin to know Him. Brethren, true religion has many sides to it; true religion is practical, it is also contemplative; but it is not true religion at all if it is not full of love and affection. Jesus must reign in your heart, or else, though you may give Him what place you like in your head, you have not truly received Him.

To Jesus, beyond all others, is applicable this title of the Beloved, for they who know Him love Him. Aye, if ever love had emphasis in it, it is the love which true believers give to Christ.

Our love to Jesus begins with trust. We experience His goodness, and then we love Him in return. "We love him because he first loved us." They say that love is blind; I should think it is, from what I have seen of it in some people; but love to Christ might have ten thousand eyes, and yet be justified in loving Him. The more you see Him, the more you know Him, the more you live with Him, the more reason will you have for loving Him.

There will never come a time in which you will have to question whether you were right to surrender your heart to Him; but even throughout the eternal ages you shall, in the felicities of His blessed company, feel that you were, in fact, more than justified in calling Him your Beloved.

This is the first part of the name the spouse gives to her Lord; no, not the *first;* the first part of the name is *"my,"* she calls him *"my Beloved."*

Brethren, this signifies appropriation; so that the two words together mean affection and appropriation: *"My Beloved."* If nobody else loves Him, I do. This is a distinguishing affection; and I love Him because He belongs to me; He is mine, He has given Himself to me; and I have chosen Him because He first chose me; He is "my Beloved." I am not ashamed to put Him in front of all others; and when men say, "What is thy Beloved more than another beloved?" I can tell them that "My Beloved" is more than all the earthly beloveds put together.

It is a delightful thing to get hold of Christ with both hands, as Thomas did when he said, "My Lord and my God." There he held Him with a double-handed grip, and would not let Him go. It is sweet and saving even to come into contact with Him, as the woman did who touched the fringe of His garment; but, oh, to take Him in your arms, to hold Him with both hands, and say, "This Christ is mine; by a daring faith, warranted by the Word of God, I take this Christ to be mine, to have and to hold, for better or worse, and neither life nor death shall ever part me from Him who is 'my Beloved.' "

Now, there is a sweet name for the Lord Jesus Christ. My dear hearers, can you speak to Jesus in that way, "My Beloved"? He who can, by the Spirit of God, say this, has uttered two words that have more eloquence in them than there is in all the orations of Demosthenes. He who cannot truly say this, though he may speak with the tongues of men and of angels, yet, since he hath not this charity, this divine love in his heart, it profiteth him nothing. Oh, that every one of you could say, "My Beloved! My Beloved!"

Do you all really know what saving faith is? It is the appropriation to one's self of Christ in His true and proper character as God has revealed Him. Canst thou make this appropriation? "Oh," says one, "I am afraid I should be stealing salvation if I did!" Listen: so long as thou canst get Christ anyhow, thou mayest have Him. There is never any stealing of that which is freely given. The difficulty is not about any rights that thou hast, for thou hast no rights whatever in this matter, but come and take what God gives to thee, though thou hast no claim to it.

Soul, take Christ tonight, and if thou takest Him, thou shalt never lose Him. I was going to say, if thou dost even steal Him, so long as thou dost but take Him to thyself, He will never withdraw Himself from thy grasp. It is written, "Him that cometh to me, I will in no wise cast out." Some come properly, and Christ does not cast them out; but there are some who come improperly, they come, as it were, limping on a wooden leg, or perhaps only creeping or crawling.

It does not matter how you come to Christ, as long as you really do come to Him, He will never cast you out. Get to Him anyhow you can; and if you once come to Him, you may plead that blessed promise of His, "Him that cometh to me I will in no wise cast out."

I have told you before that, some years ago, I felt a great depression of spirit; I knew whom I had believed; but, somehow, I could not get the comfort out of the truth I preached. I even began to wonder whether I was really saved; and, having a holiday, and being away from home, I went to the Wesleyan Chapel, and a local preacher occupied the pulpit that morning. While he preached a sermon full of the gospel, the tears flowed from my eyes, and I was in such a perfect delirium of joy on hearing the gospel, which I so seldom have an opportunity of doing, that I said, "Oh, yes, there is spiritual life within me, for the gospel can touch my heart, and stir my soul." When I went to thank the good man for his sermon, he looked at me, and he could hardly believe his eyes. He said, "Are you not Mr. Spurgeon?" I replied, "Yes." "Dear, dear," said he, "why, that is your sermon that I preached this morning!" Yes, I knew it was, and that was one reason why I was so comforted by it, because I felt that I could take my own physic, and I said to myself, "There now, that which I have seen to have a certain effect upon others has had the same effect upon me."

I asked the preacher to my inn to dinner, and we rejoiced together to think that he should have been led to give the people one of my sermons so that I should be fed out of my own cupboard. I do know this, that, whatever I may be, there is nothing that moves me like the gospel of Christ. Do not many of you feel just as I do?

II. Now I will lead you on to the second division of my subject. I have shown you what the Church calls her Lord; now, in the second place, I will tell you WHENCE SHE CALLS HIM: "Make haste, my Beloved, and be Thou like to a roe or to a young hart upon the mountains of spices." What does that mean? She cries to Him to come from the place where He now is, which she calls "the mountains of spices."

Readers of Solomon's Song know that there are four mountains spoken of in this Song. The first set of mountains is mentioned in the seventeenth verse of the second chapter of the Song, where we read of *the mountains of division:* "Until the day break, and the shadows flee away, turn, my beloved, and be thou like a roe or a young hart upon the mountains of Bether," or, the mountains of division, the divided crags, or the mountains that divide.

Well now, beloved, this was Christ's first coming. There were mountains of division; our sins and God's justice, like great mountains, divided us. How could God's love ever come to us, or how could we get to it? There were mountains of division; and, as we looked at them, we said, "They are impassable; nobody can ever climb those lofty crags, or scale those awful precipices, or cross those dread abysses." These mountains effectually separate a guilty soul from a holy God; and, my brethren, there was no way over those hills, till Jesus came like a roe or a young hart.

Roes and harts can stand on crags where men's heads turn giddy and they fall; and our Divine Master was able to stand where we could not. He came leaping over the mountains of our sins, and over the hills of divine justice, and He came even to us, and opened up a way over the mountains of Bether, the mountains of division, by which God comes to us and we come to God; and now, instead of division, there is a sacred union.

That was Christ's first coming, over the mountains of division.

But there were other mountains beside these which you read of a little further on in the Song; these were *the mountains of the leopards,* the dens of the lions. Turn to the fourth chapter, at the eighth verse; "Come with me from Lebanon, my spouse, with me from Lebanon: look from the top of Amana, from the top of Shenir and Hermon, from the lions' dens, from the mountains of the leopards."

When Christ came the first time, He met with fierce opposition, from sin, and death, and hell. These were the lions; these were the leopards; and our great Champion had to go hunting them, and they hunted Him. You know how these grim lions met Him, and how they tore Him; they rent His hands, and His feet, and His side. Do you not remember how that great lion of the pit came leaping upon Him, how He received him upon His breast, like a greater Samson, and though He fell in the death-struggle, He tore that lion asunder, as though he had been a kid, and cast him down?

As for His other enemies, He could truly say, "O death, where is thy sting? O grave, where is thy victory?" Our Well-beloved came to us, over the mountains of the leopards and the dens of the lions, more than conqueror through the greatness of His love. Do you not see Him as He comes from Edom, with dyed garments from Bozrah, traveling in the greatness of His strength, speaking in righteousness, mighty to save? In spite of all opposition, He finished the work of our redemption.

So Jesus came to us, over the mountains of separation, and over the mountains of the leopards.

But there is a third mountain mentioned in this wonderful poetical Book, and that is, *the mountain of myrrh*. In the sixth chapter at the second verse, it says, "My Beloved is gone down into His garden, to the beds of spices, to feed in the gardens, and to gather lilies." It is called a garden, but in the sixth verse of the fourth chapter it is called a mountain: "Until the day break, and the shadows flee away, I will get me to the mountain of myrrh, and to the hill of frankincense."

You know the story well. After Jesus had come over the mountains of our sins, after He had killed the lions and the leopards that stood in our way, He gave up His soul into His Father's hands, and loving friends took His body, and wrapped it in white linen, and Joseph of Arimathaea and Nicodemus brought myrrh and aloes to preserve His blessed body, that matchless casket of a perfect soul; and, having wrapped Him up, they laid Him in a new tomb, which thus became the garden or mountain of myrrh.

A bitter thing was that grave wherein He buried all our sin, that grave out of which He came victorious over death, that grave out of which He rose that He might justify His people. That was the mountain of myrrh to which Jesus went for a very brief season. Scarcely three days was He there; but I think I can hear His Church standing at the tomb, and saying,

"Make haste, my Beloved! Be Thou like a roe, or a young hart, and come quickly from Thy sleep with the dead in the mountains of myrrh."

It was but a short time that He was there, even as He said to His disciples, "A little while, and ye shall not see me; and again a little while, and ye shall see me." Soon was that slumber over, and when He woke, as Samson carried away the gate of Gaza, so Christ arose, and took up the gates of death, posts and bar and all, and carried them away, and neither death nor hell can ever bring them back again. By the resurrection of Christ, the tomb is opened, never to be closed again.

The "mountain of myrrh" is the third that is mentioned in the Song; but our text refers to *the mountains of spices.* I am not stretching this passage, or drawing a lesson where there is none; the mountains of spices are those places where Jesus dwells at this very moment at the right hand of God. It is from there that we now call Him with the spouse when she said, "Make haste, my Beloved, and be thou like to a roe or to a young hart upon the mountains of spices."

What are these spices? Are they not Christ's infinite merits, which perfume heaven and earth? The foul corruption of our sins is not perceptible, because of the mountains of spices. One single sin would be vile enough to pollute a universe; what, then, were all our sins put together? Behold this wondrous sanitary power of divine grace; these mountains of spices more than nullify the foulness of our sins. Christ's merit is perpetually before the eye of His Father, so that no longer does He perceive our sins.

What shall I say next of these mountains of spices? Are they not our Lord's perpetual and prevailing

prayers? He intercedes for His people before the throne
of God. He is that great Angel from whose swinging
censer there goes up continually the incense of intercession. The prayers of saints are presented by Him
to the Father with all His own merit added to them.
These are the mountains of spices, Christ's infinite
merits, and His ceaseless prayers, His undying suppli-
cations to the great Father on behalf of all His people.

In consequence of this, I think I may say that the
praises of His glorified people, the sweet music of the
harps of the redeemed, the everlasting symphonies of
the spirits of just men made perfect, and cleansed by
His atoning blood—are not these as sweet spices before
God? Yea, all heaven is perfumed with everything that
is precious and acceptable, full of a sweet savour unto
God, and a delightful fragrance to all His people.

Now, this is where Jesus is now; not here in this
foul, polluted world, but up yonder He rests in the
mountains of spices; and the prayer of His Church
continually is, "Come, my Beloved! Make haste, my
Beloved! Be thou like to a roe or to a young hart upon
the mountains of spices."

III. That brings me to what is really the gist, the
main point, the arrow-head of the text. We have
noticed what the Church calls her Lord, and whence
she calls Him; now, thirdly, note HOW SHE CALLS HIM.
She says, "Make haste, my Beloved, make haste."

Why is it that all the Church of God, and each in-
dividual Christian in particular, should be found anxious
for the speedy coming of our Lord Jesus Christ? I think,
surely, that *this is the result of true love*. Does not
love always wish to see the object on which its heart
is fixed? When your dearest one parts from you for

a while, do you not always wish for a speedy return? The parting is painful; it were bitter indeed if you did not expect to meet again. So you say, "Be no longer absent than you are forced to be. Come home as speedily as you can."

Where there is great love, there gets to be great longing; and that longing sometimes becomes so vehement as to be well-nigh impatient. May not the Church that mourns her absent Lord sigh and cry till He returns? Is not this the very language of intense love, "Make haste, my Beloved, and return to me"? If we love our Lord, we shall long for His appearing; be you sure of that, it is the natural result of ardent affection.

But, notwithstanding this, beloved, we sometimes need certain incentives to stir up our souls to cry for our Lord's return. One reason that ought to make the believer long for Christ's coming is that *it will end this conflict.*

Our lot is cast in a wretched time, when many things are said and done that grieve and vex God's Holy Spirit, and all who are in sympathy with Him. Sometimes, it is false doctrine that is proclaimed; and if you preach the truth, they smite you on the mouth, and then you say to yourself, "Would God the Lord would come!"

At other times, it is sheer blasphemy that is uttered, when men say, "The Lord delayeth His coming," or when they talk as if He were not Lord, as if His gospel were no gospel, and His salvation were worn out. Then we say, "Make no tarrying, O our God! Come, Lord, and tarry not!" We grow impatient then for His coming.

And, dear friend, when you see the oppression of
the poor, when you hear the cry of the needy, when
you know that many of them are ground down to
bitter poverty, and yet are struggling hard to earn a
bare pittance, you say, "Lord, will this state of things
always exist? Shall not these wrongs be righted? Oh,
that He would come, who will judge the people right-
eously and vindicate the cause of the poor and the op-
pressed!"

Then we look even on the professing church, and
we see how lukewarm it is, how honeycombed it is with
heresy and worldliness, and how often the church that
ought to honor Christ insults Him, and He is wounded
in the house of His friends. We say, "Will not this
evil soon be at an end? Will not the conflict speedily
be over?"

Oh, how have I stood, in the midst of the battle,
when the deadly shafts have flown about me on the
right hand and on the left, and, wounded full sore,
I have cried, "Will not the King Himself soon come,
and shall I not ere long hear the sound of those blessed
feet, whose every step means victory, and whose presence
is eternal life?" "Come, Lord! Make haste, my Beloved! Come to the rescue of Thy weak and feeble
servants; come, come, come, we beseech Thee!"

Put yourself into this great fight for the faith; and if
you have to bear the brunt of the battle, you will soon
be as eager as I am that Jesus should make haste, and
come to your relief. You also will cry, "Make haste,
my Beloved," when you think what wonders He will
work at His coming.

What will Christ do at His coming? *He will raise
the dead.* Mine eyes shall see Him in that day. "I

know that my Redeemer liveth, and that He shall stand, at the latter day upon the earth, and though after my skin worms destroy this body, yet in my flesh shall I see God." When Christ shall come the second time, and that blast, of which we sang just now, "the loudest and the last," shall ring through earth and heaven, then shall the dead men arise.

There are newly-made graves; the mourners' tears are not yet wiped away. There are the graves of many who have gone home long ago, and we remember them, and we say, "Would God that Christ would come, and spoil death of those precious relics! Oh, that He would reanimate those bodies, and call together the dry bones, and bid them live!" Come, Lord! Come, Lord! make no tarrying, we beseech Thee!

And when He comes, beloved, remember that *then shall be the time of the glory of His people:* "Then shall the righteous shine forth as the sun in the kingdom of their Father." Slander will be rolled away in the day when Christ cometh. The wicked shall awake to everlasting contempt, but the righteous to an everlasting justification. They shall be clear of every accusation in that day, and then shall they sit on the throne with their Lord.

They were with Him in His humiliation; they shall be with Him in His glory. They, too, were despised and rejected of men, as He was; but in that day none shall dare to despise them, for every saint shall be seen to be a king, and a son of the King. Oh, the glory that awaits His people in the day of His coming! "It doth not yet appear what we shall be: but we know that, when He shall appear, we shall be like Him;

for we shall see Him as He is." Well may the child
of God say, "Make haste, my Beloved."

Oh, for the sheathing of the sword, and the waving
of the palm! Oh, for the drying of the tear, and the
handling of the harp of gold! Oh, for the ending of
the doubt and the trouble, and the beginning of the
everlasting enjoyment and the eternal serenity at the
right hand of the Ever-blessed One!

Still, there is another reason why we say, "Make
haste, my Beloved." It is this. We desire to share in
Christ's glory; but *our chief desire is that our Lord may
be glorified*. I do believe I shall have the support of
every Christian heart when I say that we would a
thousand times rather that Christ were glorified than
that we should be honored.

Many years ago, after the Surrey Music Hall accident,
I well-nigh lost my reason through distress of heart.
I was broken down in spirit, and thought that, perhaps,
I might never preach again. I was but a young man,
and it was a great sorrow that crushed me into the
dust through that terrible accident; but one passage of
Scripture brought me recovery in a moment. I was
alone, and as I was thinking, this text came to my mind,
"Him hath God exalted with His right hand to be
a Prince and a Saviour," and I said to myself, "Is that
so? Is Jesus Christ exalted? Then I do not care if I
die in a ditch. If Christ is exalted to be a Prince and a
Saviour, that is enough for me."

I distinctly recollect remembering what is recorded of
some of Napoleon's soldiers, who were well-nigh cut
to pieces, lying dying, bleeding, suffering, agonizing on
the battle-field, but when the Emperor rode by, every
man lifted himself up as best he could, some resting

on the only arm that was left, just to look at him once more, and shout, *"Vive l'Emperor!"* The Emperor had come along, he was all right, and that was enough for his faithful followers.

I think that I felt just like that; whatever happened to me, it was true of Christ, "Him hath God exalted." Never mind what becomes of the man, the King lives and reigns, Jesus Christ is glorified; and so long as that is the case, what matters it what becomes of us? I think I can say for you, as well as for myself, that, if there is anything in this world that will glorify Christ, you will make no hesitation about the bargain. If it will glorify Christ, you say, let it come. Though your name should be cast out as evil, and your body should be left unburied, to be gnawed of dogs, what matters it, so long as He who loved us, and gave Himself for us, should ride on conquering and to conquer in the midst of the sons of men?

To every loyal soldier of King Jesus, this is the best thought in connection with His Second Advent, that when He comes, it will be to be admired in His saints, and to be glorified in all them that believe. Then shall there be universal acclamations to Him, and His enemies shall hide their heads in shame and dismay. Oh, what will they do then? What will they do in that day of His appearing? They also will live again, and what will they do in that day?

Judas, where are you? Come here, man! Sell your Lord again for thirty pieces of silver! What does he say? Why, he flees, and wishes that he could again go out, and destroy himself; but that is impossible. Now Pilate, vacillating Pilate, wash your hands in water, and say, "I am innocent of the blood of this just Person." There is no water for him to wash his hands in, and he dare not again perform that wicked farce.

And now, ye who cried, "Crucify him, crucify him," lift up your voices again if you dare! Not a dog doth move his tongue; but hearken, they have found their tongues, and what do they say? They are imploring the hills to fall upon them, they are calling on the rocks to hide them. The King has not put His hand upon His sword, He has not sent forth His lightnings to scatter you; why flee ye so, ye cravens? Hear their bitter wail! "Oh, rocks and hills, hide us from the face, from the face, from the face of Him that sitteth upon the throne!"

It is the face of Jesus, which they were bidden to look upon, that they might live; but now, in another state, they dare not look upon that face of placid love which, in that day, shall be more stern than the frowning brow of vengeance itself. Yes, they flee, they flee; but you who have trusted Christ, you whom He hath saved, you will draw near to Him, you will shout His praises, you will delight in Him, it shall be your heaven to bless Him for ever and ever. Oh, yes, great Master, "Make haste, my Beloved, and be thou like to a roe or to a young hart upon the mountains of spices," and all His saints, with one voice and heart, will say, "Amen."

Oh, that you, who have never trusted Him, would trust Him now; and if you trust Him, you shall live with Him for ever and ever. God grant it! Amen.

Chapter V

CITIZENSHIP IN HEAVEN

"For our conversation is in heaven; from whence also we look for the Saviour, the Lord Jesus Christ" (Philippians 3:20).

THERE CAN BE NO comparison between a soaring seraph and a crawling worm. Christian men ought so to live that it were idle to speak of a comparison between them and the men of the world. It should not be a comparison but a contrast. No scale of degrees should be possible; the believer should be a direct and manifest contradiction to the unregenerate. The life of a saint should be altogether above, and out of the same list as the life of a sinner. We should compel our critics not to confess that moralists are good, and Christians a little better; but while the world is darkness, we should manifestly be light; and while the world lieth in the Wicked One, we should most evidently be of God, and overcome the temptations of that Wicked One.

Wide as the poles asunder, are life and death, light and darkness, health and disease, purity and sin, spiritual and carnal, divine and sensual. If we were what we profess to be, we should be as distinct a people in the midst of this world, as a white race in a community of Ethiopians; there should be no more difficulty in detecting the Christian from the worldling than in discovering a sheep from a goat, or a lamb from a wolf.

Alas! the Church is so much adulterated, that we have
to abate our glorying, and cannot exalt her character
as we would. "The precious sons of Zion, comparable
to fine gold, how are they esteemed as earthen pitchers,
the work of the hands of the potter!" O for the time
when "our conversation shall be in heaven," and the
ignoble life of the man, whose god is his belly and
whose end is destruction, shall be rebuked by our un-
worldly, unselfish character.

There should be as much difference between the
worldling and the Christian as between hell and heaven,
between destruction and eternal life. As we hope at
last that there shall be a great gulf separating us from
the doom of the impenitent, there should be here a deep
and wide gulf between us and the ungodly. The purity
of our character should be such that men must take
knowledge of us that we are of another and superior
race. God grant us more and more to be most clearly a
chosen generation, a royal priesthood, a holy nation,
a peculiar people, that we may shew forth the praises
of Him who has called us out of darkness into His
marvelous light.

Brethren, tonight I exhort you to holiness, not by the
precepts of the law: not by the thunderings from Sinai;
not by the perils or punishments which might fall upon
you if you are unholy; but by the privileges to which
you have been admitted. Gracious souls should only
be urged by arguments from grace. Whips are for the
backs of fools, and not for heirs of heaven. By the
honorable citizenship which has been bestowed upon
you, I shall beseech you to let your conversation be in
heaven, and I shall urge that most prevailing argument,
that the Lord Jesus Christ cometh, and therefore we

should be as men that watch for our Lord, diligently doing service unto Him, that when He cometh He may say unto us, "Well done, good and faithful servants." I know that the grace which is in you will freely answer to such a plea.

Our text, I think, might be best translated thus— "Our citizenship is in heaven." The French translation renders it, "As for us, our burgess-ship is in the heavens." Doddridge paraphrases it, "But we converse as citizens of heaven, considering ourselves as denizens of the New Jerusalem, and only strangers and pilgrims upon earth."

I. The first idea which is suggested by the verse under consideration is this: if our citizenship be in heaven, then WE ARE ALIENS HERE; we are strangers and foreigners, pilgrims and sojourners in the earth, as all our fathers were. In the words of Sacred Writ "Here we have no continuing city," but "we desire a better country, that is an heavenly." Let us illustrate our position. A certain young man is sent out by his father to trade on behalf of the family: he is sent to America, and he is just now living in New York. A very fortunate thing it is for him that his citizenship is in England; that, though he lives in America and trades there, yet he is an alien, and does not belong to that afflicted nation; for he retains his citizenship with us on this side the Atlantic. Yet there is a line of conduct which is due from him to the country which affords him shelter, and he must see to it that he does not fail to render it.

Since *we* are aliens, we must remember to behave ourselves as aliens should, and by no means come short in our duty. We are affected by the position of our

temporary country. A person trading in New York or
Boston, though a freeman of the city of London, will
find himself very much affected by the trade of the
Dis-United States; when the merchants of his city suffer,
he will find himself suffering with them, the fluctuations
of their money-market will affect his undertakings, and
the stagnation of commerce will slacken his progress;
but if prosperity should happily return, he will find that
when the coffers of their merchants are getting full,
his will be the better; and the happy development of
trade will give buoyancy to his own ventures. He is
not of the nation, and yet every trembling of the scale
will affect him; he will prosper as that nation prospers,
and he will suffer as that nation suffers; that is to say,
not as a citizen, but as a trader.

And so we in this country find that though we are
strangers and foreigners on earth, yet we share all the
inconveniences of the flesh. No exception is granted
to us from the common lot of manhood. We are born
to trouble, even as others, and have tribulation like the
rest. When famine comes we hunger; and when war
rages we are in danger; exposed to the same clime,
bearing the same burning heat, or the same freezing
cold; we know the whole train of ills, even as the citizens of earth know them.

Seeking the good of the country as aliens, we must
also remember that it behooves aliens to *keep themselves
very quiet*. What business have foreigners to plot
against the government, or to intermeddle with the
politics of a country in which they have no citizenship?
An Englishman in New York had best be without a
tongue just now; if he should criticize the courage of
the generals, the accuracy of their despatches, or the

genius of the President, he might meet with rather rough usage. He will be injudicious indeed, if he cannot leave America to the Americans. So, in this land of ours, when you and I are strangers, we must be orderly sojourners, submitting ourselves constantly to those that are in authority, leading orderly and peaceable lives, and, according to the command of the Holy Ghost through the apostle, "honoring all men, fearing God, honoring the king"; "submitting ourselves to every ordinance of man for the Lord's sake."

I cannot say that I delight in political Christians; I fear that party-strife is a serious trial of believers, and I cannot reconcile our heavenly citizenship with the schemes of the hustings and the riot of the polling-booth. You must follow your own judgment here, but for my part, I am a foreigner even in England, and as such, I mean to act. We are simply passing through this earth, and should bless it in our transit, but never yoke ourselves to its affairs. An Englishman may happen to be in Spain—he wishes a thousand things were different from what they are, but he does not trouble himself much about them: says he, "If I were a Spaniard I would see what I could do to alter this government, but, being an Englishman, let the Spaniards see to their own matters. I shall be back to my own country by-and-by, and the sooner the better."

So with Christians here; they are content very much to let the potsherds strive with the potsherds of the earth; their politics concern their own country, they do not care much about any other; as *men* they love liberty, and are not willing to lose it even in the lower sense; but, spiritually, their politics are spiritual, and as citizens they look to the interest of that divine republic to which

they belong, and they wait for the time when, having
patiently borne with the laws of the land of their banishment, they shall come under the more beneficent sway
of him who reigns in glory, the King of kings, and
Lord of lords. If it be possible, as much as lieth in
you, live peaceably with all men, and serve your day
and generation still, but build not your soul's dwelling
place here, for all this earth must be destroyed at the
coming of the fiery day.

As we are free from the conscription of the State,
we must remember, also, that we are *not eligible to its
honors.* I know you will say that is not a privilege; but
it is a great boon if looked at aright. An Englishman
in New York is not eligible for the very prickly throne
of the President; I suppose he could not well be made
a governor of Massachusetts or any other State, and,
indeed, he may be well content to renounce the dif-
ficulties and the honor too.

So also, the Christian man here is not eligible to this
world's honors. It is a very ill omen to hear the Christian man. He may begin to look to his standing, and
wonder whether he has not been doing wrong when
the unrighteous give him their approbation. "What,
did I do wrong," said Socrates, "that yonder villain
praised me just now?" And so may the Christian say,
"What, have I done wrong, that So-and-so spoke well
of me, for if I had done right he would not; he has
not the sense to praise goodness, he could only have
applauded that which suited his own taste."

Christian men, ye must never covet the world's es-
teem; the love of this world is not in keeping with the
love of God. "If any man love the world the love of
the Father is not in him." Treat its smiles as you treat

its threats, with quiet contempt. Be willing rather to be sneered at than to be approved, counting the cross of Christ greater riches than all the treasures of Egypt.

O harlot world, it were a sad dishonor to be thy favorite. Tire thy head and paint thy face, thou Jezebel, but thou art no friend of ours, nor will we desire thy hollow love. The men of this world were mad to raise us to their seats of honor, for we are aliens and citizens of another country. When the Pope sent a noted Protestant statesman a present of some silver goblets, he returned them with this answer — "The citizens of Zurich compel their judges to swear twice in the year that they will receive no presents from foreign princes, therefore take them back."

More than twice in the year should the Christian resolve that he will not accept the smiles of this world, and will do no homage to its glory. "We fear the Greeks even when they bear gifts." Like the Trojans of old, we may be beguiled with presents even if unconquered in arms. Forswear then the grandeur and honor of this fleeting age. Say in life, what a proud cardinal said in death. "Vain pomp and glory of the world, I hate ye." Pass through Vanity-Fair without trading in its vanities; crying, in answer to their "What will ye buy?"—"We buy the truth."

A certain minister, collecting for a chapel, called upon a rich merchant who generously gave him fifty pounds. As the good man was going out with sparkling eye at the liberality of the merchant, the tradesman opened a letter, and he said, "Stop a minute, I find by this letter I have lost this morning a ship worth six thousand pounds." The poor minister trembled in his shoes, for he thought the next word would be, "Let me have the fifty pound check back." Instead of it, it was "Let me have the check back a moment," and then taking out his pen he wrote him a check for five hundred pounds. "As my money is going so fast, it is well," said he, "to make sure of some of it, so I will put some of it in God's bank." The man, you doubt not, went his way astonished at such a way of dealing as this, but indeed that is just what a man should do, who feels he is an alien here, and his treasure is beyond the sky.

II. It is our comfort now to remind you that although aliens *on earth,* WE ARE CITIZENS IN HEAVEN.

What is meant by our being citizens in heaven? Why, first that *we are under heaven's government.* Christ the king of heaven reigns in our hearts; the laws of glory are the laws of our consciences; our daily prayer is, "Thy will be done on earth, as it is in heaven." The proclamations issued from the throne of glory are freely received by us, the decrees of the Great King we cheerfully obey. We are not without law to Christ. The Spirit of God rules in our mortal bodies, grace reigns through righteousness, and we wear the easy yoke of Jesus. O that He would sit as king in our hearts, like Solomon upon his throne of gold. Thine are we, Jesus, and all that we have; rule thou without a rival.

As citizens of the New Jerusalem, *we share heaven's honors.* The glory which belongs to beatified saints belongs to us, for we are already sons of God, already princes of the blood imperial; already we wear the spotless robe of Jesus' righteousness; already we have angels for our servitors, saints for our companions, Christ for our brother, God for our Father, and a crown of immortality for our reward. We share the honors of citizenship, for we have come to the general assembly and Church of the firstborn, whose names are written in heaven. "Beloved, now are we the sons of God, and it doth not yet appear what we shall be: but we know that, when he shall appear, we shall be like him; for we shall see him as he is."

As citizens, *we have common rights in all the property of heaven.* Those wide extensive plains we sung of just now are ours; ours yon harps of gold and crowns of glory; ours the gates of pearl and walls of chrysolite; ours the azure light of the city that needs no candle nor light of the sun; ours the river of the water of life, and the twelve manner of fruits which grow on the trees planted at the side thereof; there is nought in heaven that belongeth not unto us, for our citizenship is there. "Things present, or things to come; all are ours; and we are Christ's; and Christ is God's."

And as we are thus under heaven's government, and share its honors and partake of its possessions, so we today *enjoy its delights.* Do they rejoice over sinners that are born to God—prodigals that have returned? So do we. Do they chant the glories of triumphant grace? We do the same. Do they cast their crowns at Jesus' feet? Such honors as we have, we cast there too. Do they rejoice in Him? So also do we. Do they triumph, waiting for His second advent? By faith we triumph in the same. Are they tonight singing "Worthy the Lamb"? We also have sung the same tune, not to such glorious notes as theirs, but with as sincere hearts; with minstrelsy not quite so splendid, but we hope as sincere, for the Spirit gave us the music which we have, and the Spirit gave them the thunders of their acclamations before the throne. "Our citizenship is in heaven."

Brethren, we rejoice to know also that as the result of our being citizens, or rather I ought to have said as the cause of it, our *names are written in the roll* of heaven's free-men. When, at last, the list shall be read, our names shall be read too; for where Paul and Peter, where David and Jonathan, where Abraham and Jacob shall be found, we shall be found too; numbered with them we were in the divine purpose, reckoned with them we were in the purchase on the cross, and with them shall we sit down for ever at the tables of the blessed. The small and the great are fellow-citizens and of the same household. The babes and the perfect men are recorded in the same great registry, and neither death nor hell can erase a single name.

Our citizenship then is in heaven. We have not time to extend that thought. John Calvin says of this text, "It is a most abundant source of many exhortations, which it were easy for any one to elicit from it." We are not all Calvins; but even to our smaller capacities, the subject appears to be one not readily exhausted, but rich with unfathomable joy.

III. We must now come to our third point, which is, OUR CONVERSATION IS IN HEAVEN, our walk and acts are such as are consistent with our dignity *as citizens of heaven*. Among the old Romans, when a dastardly action was proposed it was thought a sufficient refusal to answer "Romanus sum—I am a Roman." Surely it should be a strong incentive to every good thing if we can claim to be freemen of the Eternal City. Let our lives be conformed to the glory of our citizenship. In heaven they are holy, so must we be—so are we if our citizenship is not a mere pretence. They are happy, so must we be rejoicing in the Lord always.

In heaven they are obedient, so must we be, following the faintest monitions of the divine will. In heaven they are active, so should we be, both day and night praising and serving God. In heaven they are peaceful, so should we find a rest in Christ and be at peace even now. In heaven they rejoice to behold the face of Christ, so should we be always meditating upon Him, studying His beauties, and desiring to look into the truths which He has taught. In Heaven they are full of love, so should we, who though many, are one body, be every one members one of the other.

Before the throne they are free from envy and strife, ill-will, jealousy, emulation, falsehood, anger, so should we be: we should, in fact, seek while we are here to keep up the manners and customs of the good old fatherland, so that, as in Paris, the Parisian soon says, "There goes John Bull," so they should be able to say in this land, "There goes a heavenly citizen, one who is with us, and among us, but is not of us." Our very speech should be such that our citizenship should be detected. We should not be able to live long in a house without men finding out what we are.

A friend of mine once went across to America, and landing I think at Boston, he knew nobody, but hearing a man say, when somebody had dropped a cask on the quay, "Look out there, or else you will make a Coggeshall job of it," he said, "You are an Essex man I know, for that is a proverb never used anywhere but in Essex: give me your hand"; and they were friends at once. So there should be a ring of true metal about our speech and conversation, so that when a brother meets us, he can say "You are a Christian, I know, for none but Christians speak like that, or act like that."

"Thou also wast with Jesus of Nazareth, for thy speech bewrayeth thee." Our holiness should act as a sort of freemasonry by which we know how to give the grip to the stranger, who is not a real stranger, but a fellow-citizen with us, and of the household of faith.

Oh! dear friends, wherever we wander, we should never forget our beloved land. In Australia, on the other side the world, or in the Cape of Good Hope, or wherever else we may be exiled, surely every Englishman's eye must turn to this fair island; and with all her faults, we must love her still. And surely let us be where we may, our eyes must turn to heaven, the happy land unstained by shadow of fault; we love her still, and love her more and more, praying for the time when our banishment shall expire, and we shall enter into our fatherland to dwell there for ever and ever. Shenstone says, "The proper means of increasing the love we bear our native country, is to reside some time in a foreign land." Sure am I that we who cry, "Woe is me, for I dwell in Mesech, and sojourn in the tents of Kedar!" are sure to add "Oh, that I had wings like a dove, for then would I fly away, and be at rest."

IV. The text says, "Our conversation is in heaven," and I think we may read it, as though it said, "OUR COMMERCE IS IN HEAVEN." We are trading on earth, but still the bulk of our trade is with heaven. We trade for trinkets in this land, but our gold and silver are in heaven. We commune with heaven, and how? Our trade is with heaven by *meditation;* we often think of God our Father, and Christ our Brother; and, by the Spirit, the Comforter, we are brought in contemplative delight, to the general assembly and Church of the firstborn, whose names are written in heaven.

Brethren, do not our *thoughts* sometimes burn within us, when we trade with that blessed land? When I have sent the ships of understanding and consideration to that land of Ophir, which is full of gold, and they have come back again laden with all manner of precious things, my thoughts have been enriched, my soul has longed to journey to that good land. Black and stormy art thou, O sea of death, but I would cross thee to reach that land of Havilah, which hath dust of gold. I know that he who is a Christian will never have his mind long off that better land. And do you know we sometimes trade with heaven in our *hymns?*

They tell us of the Swiss soldiery in foreign countries, that there is a song which the band is forbidden to play, because it reminds them of the cowbells of their native hills. If the men hear it, they are sure to desert, for that dear old song revives before their eyes the wooden chalets and the cows, and the pastures of the glorious Alps, and they long to be away. There are some of our hymns that make us homesick. In times of high, hallowed, heavenly harmony of praise, the songs of angels seem to come astray, and find their way down to us, and then our songs return with them, hand in hand, and go back to God's throne, through Jesus Christ.

We trade with heaven, I hope, too, not only thus by meditation, and by thought, and by song, but *by hopes and by loves.* Our love is toward that land. How heartily the Germans sing of the dear old father-land; but they cannot, with all their Germanic patriot-ism, they cannot beat the genial glow of the Briton's heart, when he thinks of his fatherland too. The Scotch-man, too, wherever he may be, remembers the land of "brown heath and shaggy wood." And the Irishman, too, let him be where he will, still thinks the "Emerald Isle" the first gem of the sea. It is right that the patriot should love his country. Does not our love fervently flame towards heaven? We think we cannot speak well enough of it, and indeed here we are correct, for no exaggeration is possible. When we talk of that land of Eschol, our mouths are watering to taste its clusters; already, like David, we thirst to drink of the well that is within the gate; and we hunger after the good corn of the land. Our ears are wanting to have done with the discords of earth, that they may open to the harmonies of heaven; and our tongues are longing to sing the melodious sonnets, sung by flaming ones above. Yes, we do love heaven, and thus it is that we prove that our commerce is with that better land.

Brethren, just as people in a foreign land that love their country always are glad to have plenty of letters from the country, I hope we have much *communication with the old fatherland*. We send our prayers there as letters to our Father, and we get His letters back in this blessed volume of His Word. You go into an Australian settler's hut, and you find a newspaper. Where from, sir? A gazette from the south of France, a journal from America? Oh no, it is a newspaper from England, addressed to him in his old mother's hand-writing, bearing the postage stamp with the good Queen's face in the corner; and he likes it, though it be only a newspaper from some little pottering country town, with no news in it; yet he likes it better, perhaps, than the "Times" itself, because it talks to him about the village where he lived, and consequently touches a special string in the harp of his soul.

So must it be with heaven. This book, the Bible, is the newspaper of heaven, and therefore we must love it. The sermons which are preached are good news from a far country. The hymns we sing are notes by which we tell our Father of our welfare here, and by which He whispers into our soul His continued love to us. All these are and must be pleasant to us, for our commerce is with heaven. I hope, too, we are sending a good deal home. I like to see our young fellows when they go out to live in the bush, recollect their mother at home. They say "She had a hard struggle to bring us up when our father died, and she scraped her little together to help us to emigrate." John and Tom mutually agree, "the first gold we get at the diggings we will send home to mother." And it goes home.

Well, I hope you are sending a great many things home. Dear friends, I hope as we are aliens here, we are not laying up our treasure here, where we may lose it, but packing it off as quickly as we can to our own country. There are many ways of doing it. God has many banks; and they are all safe ones. We have but to serve His Church, or serve the souls which Christ has bought with His blood, or help His poor, clothe His naked, and feed His hungry, and we send our treasures beyond sea in a safe ship, and so we keep up our commerce with the skies.

V. Time has gone; those clocks will strike when they ought not. There is a great reason why we should live like aliens and foreigners here, and that is, CHRIST IS COMING SOON. The early Church never forgot this. Did they not pant and thirst after the return of their ascended Lord? Like the twelve tribes, day and night they constantly watched for Messiah. But the Church has grown weary of this hope. There have been so many false prophets who tell us that Christ is coming, that the Church thinks He never will come; and she begins to deny, or to keep in the background the blessed doctrine of the second advent of her Lord from heaven.

I do not think the fact that there have been many false prophets should make us doubt our Lord's true word. Perhaps the very frequency of these mistakes may show that there is truth at the bottom. You have a friend who is ill, and the doctor says he cannot last long; he must die; you have called a great many times expecting to hear of his departure, but he is still alive; now the frequent errors of the physicians do not prove that your friend will not die one of these days, and that speedily too. And so, though the false prophets have said, "Lo, here," and "Lo, there," and yet Christ has not come, that does not prove that His glorious appearing will never arrive. You know I am no prophet. I do not know anything about 1866; I find quite enough to do to attend to 1862. I do not understand the visions of Daniel or Ezekiel; I find I have enough to do to teach the simple word such as I find in Matthew, Mark, Luke, and John, and the Epistles of Paul.

I do not find many souls have been converted to God by exquisite dissertations about the battle of Armageddon, and all those other fine things; I have no doubt prophesyings are very profitable, but I rather question whether they are so profitable to the hearers, as they may be to the preachers and publishers. I conceive that among religious people of a certain sort, the abortive explanations of prophecy issued by certain doctors gratify a craving which in irreligious people finds its food in novels and romances. People have a panting to know the future; and certain divines pander to this depraved taste, by prophesying for them, and letting them know what is coming by-and-by.

I do not know the future, and I shall not pretend to know. But I do preach this, because I know it, that *Christ will come,* for He says so in a hundred passages. The Epistles of Paul are full of the advent, and Peter's too, and John's letters are crowded with it. The best of saints have always lived on the hope of the advent. There was Enoch, he prophesied of the coming of the Son of Man. So there was another Enoch who was always talking of the coming, and saying, "Come quickly."

I will not divide the house tonight by discussing whether the advent will be pre-millennial or post-millennial, or anything of that, it is enough for me that *He will come,* and "in such an hour as ye think not, the Son of Man will come." Tonight He may appear, while here we stand; just when we think that he will not come, the thief shall break open the house. We ought, therefore, to be always watching. Since the gold and silver that you have will be worthless at His advent; since your lands and estates will melt to smoke when He appeareth; since, *then* the righteous shall be rich, and the godly shall be great, lay not up your treasure here, for it may at any time vanish, at any time disappear, for Christ may at any moment come.

I think the Church would do well to be always living as if Christ might come today. I feel persuaded she is doing ill if she works as if He would not come till 1866, because He may come before, and He may come this moment. Let her always be living as if He would come *now,* still acting in her Master's sight, and watching unto prayer. Never mind about the last vials, fill your own vial with sweet odors and offer it before the Lord. Think what you like about Armageddon, but forget not to fight the good fight of faith. Guess not at the precise era for the destruction of Antichrist, go and destroy it yourself, fighting against it every day; but be looking forward and hastening unto the coming of the Son of Man; and let this be at once your comfort and excitement to diligence—that the Saviour will soon come from heaven.

Now, I think you foreigners here present—and I hope there are a great many true aliens here—ought to feel like a poor stranded mariner on a desolate island, who has saved a few things from the wreck and built himself an old log hut, and has a few comforts round about him, but for all that he longs for home. Every morning he looks out to sea and wonders when he shall see a sail; many times while examining the wide ocean to look for a ship, he has clapped his hands, and then wept to find he was disappointed; every night he lights his fire that there may be a blaze, so that if a ship should go by, they may send relief to the stranded mariner.

Ah! that is just the way we ought to live. We have heard of one saint who used to open his window every morning when he woke, to see if Christ had come; it might be fanaticism, but better to be enthusiastic than to mind earthly things. I would have us look out each night and light the fire of prayer, that it may be burning in case the ships of heaven should go by, that blessings may come to us poor aliens and foreigners who need them so much. Let us wait patiently till the Lord's convoy shall take us on board, that we may be carried into the glories and splendor of the reign of Christ, let us always hold the log-hut with a loose hand, and long for the time when we shall get to that better land where our possessions are, where our Father lives, where our treasures lie, where all our brethren dwell. Well said our poet—

> "Blest scenes, through rude and stormy seas
> I onward press to you."

My beloved friends, I can assure you it is always one of the sweetest thoughts I ever know, that I shall meet with you in heaven. There are so many of you members of this Church, that I can hardly get to shake hands with you once in a year; but I shall have plenty of time then in heaven. You will know your pastor in heaven better than you do now. He loves you now, and you love him. We shall then have more time to recount our experience of divine grace, and praise God together, and sing together, and rejoice together concerning Him by whom we were helped to plant, and sow, and through whom all the increase came.

But we shall not all meet in glory; not all, unless you repent. Some of you will certainly perish, unless you believe in Christ. But why must we be divided? Oh, why not all in heaven? "Believe in the Lord Jesus Christ, and thou shalt be saved." "He that believeth and is baptized shall be saved, but he that believeth not shall be damned." Trust Christ, sinner, and heaven is thine, and mine, and we are safe for ever. Amen.

CHAPTER VI

"BEHOLD, HE COMETH WITH CLOUDS"

"Behold, he cometh with clouds; and every eye shall see Him, and they also which pierced him; and all kindreds of the earth shall wail because of Him. Even so, Amen" (Revelation 1:7).

IN READING THE CHAPTER we observed how the beloved John saluted the seven churches in Asia with, "Grace and peace be unto you." Blessed men scatter blessings. When the *benediction* of God rests on us we pour out benediction upon others.

From benediction John's gracious heart rose into *adoration* of the great King of Saints. As our hymn puts it, "The holy to the holiest leads." They that are good at blessing men will be quick at blessing God.

It is a wonderful doxology which John has given us: "Unto Him that loved us, and washed us from our sins in His own blood, and hath made us kings and priests unto God and His Father; to Him be glory and dominion for ever and ever. Amen." I like that Revised Version for its alliteration in this case, although I cannot prefer it for other reasons. It runs thus: "Unto him that *loveth* us, and *loosed* us from our sins by his blood." Truly our Redeemer has loosed us from sin; but the mention of His blood suggests washing rather than loosing. We can keep the alliteration and yet retain the meaning of cleansing if we read

the passage, "Unto him that loved us, and laved us."
Loved us, and *laved* us; carry those two words home
with you: let them lie upon your tongue to sweeten
your breath for prayer and praise. "Unto him that
loved us, and laved us, be glory and dominion for ever
and ever."

It would seem from the chapter that the adoration
of John was increased by his *expectation* of the Lord's
second coming; for he cries, "Behold, he cometh with
clouds." His adoration awoke his expectation, which
all the while was lying in his soul as an element of
that vehement heat of reverent love which he poured
forth in his doxology. "Behold, he cometh," said he,
and thus he revealed one source of his reverence. "Behold, he cometh," said he, and this exclamation was the
result of his reverence. He adored until his faith
realized his Lord, and became a second and nobler sight.

I think, too, that his reverence was deepened and his
adoration was rendered more fervent by his conviction
of the speediness of his Lord's coming. "Behold, he
cometh," or is coming: he means to assert that He is
even now on His way. As workmen are moved to be
more diligent in service when they hear their master's
footfall, so, doubtless, saints are quickened in their de-
votion when they are conscious that He whom they worship is drawing near. He has gone away to the Father
for a while, and so He has left us alone in this world;
but He has said, "I will come again and receive you
unto myself," and we are confident that He will keep
His word.

Sweet is the remembrance of that loving promise.
That assurance is pouring its savor into John's heart
while he is adoring; and it becomes inevitable, as well

as most meet and proper, that his doxology should at
its close introduce him to the Lord Himself, and cause
him to cry out, "Behold, he cometh." Having worshiped among the pure in heart, he sees the Lord:
having adored the King, he sees Him assume the judg-
ment-seat, and appear in the clouds of heaven. When
once we enter upon heavenly things we know not how
far we can go, nor how high we can climb. John who
began with blessing the churches now beholds his Lord.

I. May the Holy Spirit help us while, in the first
place, we remember that OUR LORD JESUS CHRIST
COMES!

This announcement is thought worthy of a note of
admiration. As the Latins would say, there is an
"*Ecce*" placed here—"*Behold*, he cometh." As in the
old books the printers put hands in the margin pointing
to special passages, such is this "Behold!" It is a *Nota
Bene* calling upon us to note well what we are reading.
Here is something which we are to *hold* and *behold*.
We now hear a voice crying, "Come and see!" The
Holy Spirit never uses superfluous words, nor redundant
notes of exclamation: when He cries, "Behold!" it is
because there is reason for deep and lasting attention.
Will you turn away when He bids you pause and
ponder, linger and look?

Oh, you that have been beholding vanity, come and
behold the fact that Jesus cometh. You that have been
beholding this, and beholding that, and thinking of
nothing worthy of your thoughts; forget these passing
sights and spectacles, and for once behold a scene which
has no parallel. It is not a monarch in her jubilee, but
the King of kings in His glory. That same Jesus who
went up from Olivet into heaven is coming again to

earth in like manner as His disciples saw Him go into heaven. Come and behold this great sight. If ever there was a thing in the world worth looking at, it is this. Behold and see if there was ever glory like unto His glory! Hearken to the midnight cry, "Behold, the Bridegroom cometh!"

It has practically to do with you. "Go ye forth to meet him." This voice is to you, O sons of men. Do not carelessly turn aside; for the Lord God Himself demands your attention: He commands you to "Behold!" Will you be blind when God bids you behold? Will you shut your eyes when your Saviour cries, "Behold"? When the finger of inspiration points the way, will not your eye follow where it directs you? "Behold, he cometh." O my hearers, look hither, I beseech you.

If we read the words of our text carefully, this "Behold" shows us first, that *this coming is to be vividly realized*. I think I see John. He is in the spirit; but on a sudden he seems startled into a keener and more solemn attention. His mind is more awake than usual, though he was ever a man of bright eyes that saw afar. We always liken him to the eagle for the height of his flight and the keenness of his vision; yet on a sudden, even he seems startled with a more astounding vision. He cries out, "Behold! Behold!" He has caught sight of his Lord. He says not, "He will come by-and-by," but, "I can see Him; He is now coming." He has evidently realized the second advent. He has so conceived of the second coming of the Lord that it has become a matter of fact to him; a matter to be spoken of, and even to be written down. "Behold, he cometh!"

Have you and I ever realized the coming of Christ so fully as this? Perhaps we believe that He will come.

I should hope that we all do *that*. If we believe that the Lord Jesus has come the first time, we believe also that He will come the second time; but are these equally assured truths to us? Peradventure we have vividly realized the first appearing: from Bethlehem to Golgotha, and from Calvary to Olivet we have traced the Lord, understanding that blessed cry, "Behold the Lamb of God, which taketh away the sin of the world!" Yes, the Word was made flesh and dwelt among us, and we beheld His glory, the glory of the Only-begotten of the Father, full of grace and truth.

But have we with equal firmness grasped the thought that He comes again without a sin-offering unto salvation? Do we now say to each other, as we meet in happy fellowship, "Yes, our Lord cometh"? It should be to us not only a prophecy assuredly believed among us, but a scene pictured in our souls, and anticipated in our hearts. My imagination has often set forth that dread scene: but better still, my faith has realized it. I have heard the chariot-wheels of the Lord's approach, and I have endeavored to set my house in order for His reception. I have felt the shadow of that great cloud which shall attend Him, damping the ardor of my worldliness. I hear even now in spirit the sound of the last trumpet, whose tremendous blast startles my soul to serious action, and puts force into my life. Would God that I lived more completely under the influence of that august event!

This coming is to be zealously proclaimed, for John does not merely calmly say, "He cometh," but he vigorously cries, "Behold, he cometh." Just as the herald of a king prefaces his message by a trumpet blast that calls attention, so John cries, "Behold!" As the old town-crier was wont to say, "O yes! O yes! O yes" or to use some other striking formula by which he called upon men to note his announcement, so John stands in the midst of us, and cries, "Behold, he cometh!" He calls attention by that emphatic word "Behold!" It is no ordinary message that he brings, and he would not have us treat his word as a commonplace saying. He throws his heart into the announcement. He proclaims it loudly, he proclaims it solemnly, and he proclaims it with authority: "Behold, he cometh."

Brethren, no truth ought to be more frequently proclaimed, next to the first coming of the Lord, than His second coming; and you cannot thoroughly set forth all the ends and bearings of the first advent if you forget the second. At the Lord's Supper, there is no discerning the Lord's body unless you discern His first coming; but there is no drinking into His cup to its fulness, unless you hear Him say, "Until I come." You must look forward, as well as backward.

So must it be with all our ministries; they must look to Him on the cross and on the throne. We must vividly realize that He, who has once come, is coming yet again, or else our testimony will be marred, and one-sided. We shall make lame work of preaching and teaching if we leave out either advent.

And next, *it is to be unquestionably asserted.* "Behold, he cometh." It is not, "Perhaps He will come"; nor, "Peradventure He may yet appear." "Behold, he cometh" should be dogmatically asserted as an absolute certainty, which has been realized by the heart of the man who proclaims it. "Behold, he cometh." All the prophets say that He will come. From Enoch down to

the last that spoke by inspiration, they declare, "The
Lord cometh with ten thousands of His saints."

You shall not find one who has spoken by the authority of God, who does not, either directly or by
implication, assert the coming of the Son of man, when
the multitudes born of woman shall be summoned to
His bar to receive the recompense of their deed. All
the promises are travailing with this prognostication,
"Behold, he cometh." We have His own word for it,
and this makes assurance doubly sure. He has told us
that He will come again. He often assured His disciples that if He went away from them He would
come again to them; and He left us the Lord's Supper
as a parting token to be observed until He comes. As
often as we break bread we are reminded of the fact
that, though it is a most blessed ordinance, yet it is
a temporary one, and will cease to be celebrated when
our absent Lord is once again present with us.

What, dear brethren, is there to hinder Christ from
coming? When I have studied and thought over this
word, "Behold, he cometh," yes, I have said to myself,
indeed He does; who shall hold Him back? His heart
is with His church on earth. In the place where He
fought the battle He desires to celebrate the victory.
His delights are with the sons of men. All His saints
are waiting for the day of His appearing, and He is
waiting also. The very earth in her sorrow and her
groaning travaileth for His coming, which is to be her
redemption. The creation is made subject to vanity
for a little while; but when the Lord shall come again,
the creation itself also shall be delivered from the
bondage of corruption into the glorious liberty of the
children of God.

We might question whether He would come a second time if He had not already come the first time; but if He came to Bethlehem, be assured that His feet shall yet stand upon Olivet. If He came to die, doubt not that He will come to reign. If He came to be despised and rejected of men, why should we doubt that He will come to be admired in all them that believe? His sure coming is to be unquestionably asserted.

There is this sense lying in the background— that *He is already on the way*. All that He is doing in providence and grace is a preparation for His coming. All the events of human history, all the great decisions of His august majesty whereby He ruleth all things—all these are tending towards the day of His appearing. Do not think that He delays His coming, and then upon a sudden He will rush hither in hot haste. He has arranged for it to take place as soon as wisdom allows. We know not what may make the present delay imperative; but the Lord knows, and that suffices.

You grow uneasy because near two thousand years have passed since His ascension, and Jesus has not yet come; but you do not know what had to be arranged for, and how far the lapse of time was absolutely necessary for the Lord's designs. Those are no little matters which have filled up the great pause: the intervening centuries have teemed with wonders. A thousand things may have been necessary in heaven itself ere the consummation of all things could be arrived at.

When our Lord comes it shall be seen that He came as quickly as He could, speaking after the manner of His infinite wisdom; for He cannot behave Himself otherwise than wisely, perfectly, divinely. He cannot be moved by fear or passion so as to act hastily as you and I too often do. He dwells in the leisure of eternity, and in the serenity of Omnipotence. He has not to measure out days, and months, and years, and to accomplish so much in such a space or else leave His life-work undone; but according to the power of an endless life He proceeds steadily on, and to Him a thousand years are but as one day.

Therefore be assured that the Lord is even now coming. He is making everything tend that way. All things are working towards that grand climax. At this moment, and every moment since He went away, the Lord Jesus has been coming back again. "Behold, he cometh!" He is on the way! He is nearer every hour!

And we are told that *His coming will be attended by a peculiar sign*. "Behold, he cometh *with clouds*." We shall have no need to question whether it is the Son of man who has come, or whether He is indeed come. This is to be no secret matter: His coming will be as manifest as yonder clouds. In the wilderness the presence of Jehovah was known by a visible pillar of cloud by day, and an equally visible pillar of fire by night. That pillar of cloud was the sure token that the Lord was in His holy place, dwelling between the cherubim. Such is the token of the coming of the Lord Christ.

> "Every eye the cloud shall scan,
> Ensign of the Son of man."

So it is written, "And then shall appear the sign of the Son of man in heaven: and then shall all the tribes of the earth mourn, and they shall see the Son of man coming in the clouds of heaven with power and great glory."

I cannot quote at this time all those many passages

of Scripture in which it is indicated that our Lord will
come either sitting upon a cloud, or "with the clouds,"
or "with the clouds of heaven"; but such expressions
are abundant. Is it not to show that His coming will
be *majestic?* He maketh the clouds His chariots. He
cometh with hosts of attendants, and these of a nobler
sort than earthly monarchs can summon to do them
homage. With clouds of angels, cherubim and seraphim,
and all the armies of heaven He comes. With all the
forces of nature, thunder-cloud and blackness of tempest,
the Lord of all makes His triumphant entrance to judge
the world.

The clouds are the dust of His feet in that dread
day of battle when He shall ease Him of his adversaries,
shaking them out of the earth with His thunder, and
consuming them with the devouring flame of His lightning. All heaven shall gather with its utmost pomp to
the great appearing of the Lord, and all the terrible
grandeur of nature shall then be seen at its full. Not
as the Man of Sorrows, despised and rejected of men,
shall Jesus come; but as Jehovah came upon Sinai in the
midst of thick clouds and a terrible darkness, so shall
He come, Whose coming shall be the final judgment.

The clouds, also, denote *the terror of His coming
to the ungodly.* His saints shall be caught up together
with Him in the clouds, to meet the Lord in the air;
but to those that shall remain on earth the clouds shall
turn to blackness and horror of darkness. Then shall
the impenitent behold this dread vision—the Son of
man coming in the clouds of heaven. The clouds shall
fill them with dread, and the dread shall be abundantly
justified, for those clouds are big with vengeance, and
shall burst in judgment on their heads. His great white

throne, though it be bright and lustrous with hope to
His people, will with its very brightness and whiteness
of immaculate justice strike dead the hopes of all those
who trusted that they might live in sin and yet go un-
punished. "Behold, he cometh. He cometh with clouds."

I am in happy circumstances tonight, because my subject requires no effort of imagination from me. To indulge fancy on such a theme would be a wretched pro-
fanation of so sublime a subject, which in its own
simplicity should come home to all hearts. Think clearly
for a moment, till the meaning becomes real to you.
Jesus Christ is coming, coming in unwonted splendor.
When He comes He will be enthroned far above the
attacks of His enemies, the persecutions of the godless,
and the sneers of skeptics. He is coming in the clouds
of heaven, and we shall be among the witnesses of His
appearing. Let us dwell upon this truth.

II. Our second observation is this: OUR LORD'S COM-
ING WILL BE SEEN OF ALL. "Behold, he cometh with
clouds, *and every eye shall see him, and they also which
pierced him.*"

I gather from this expression, first, that *it will be a
literal appearing, and an actual sight.* If the second
advent was to be a spiritual manifestation, to be perceived by the minds of men, the phraseology would be,
"Every mind shall perceive Him." But it is not so: we
read, "Every eye shall see him." Now, the mind can
behold the spiritual, but the eye can only see that which
is distinctly material and visible. The Lord Jesus Christ
will not come spiritually, for in that sense He is always
here; but He will come really and substantially, for
every eye shall see Him, even those unspiritual eyes
which gazed on Him with hate, and pierced Him.

Go not away and dream, and say to yourself, "Oh, there is some spiritual meaning about all this." Do not destroy the teaching of the Holy Ghost by the idea that there will be a spiritual manifestation of the Christ of God, but that a literal appearing is out of the question. That would be altering the record. The Lord Jesus shall come to earth a second time as literally as He has come a first time. The same Christ who ate a piece of broiled fish and of a honeycomb after He had risen from the dead; the same who said, "Handle me, and see; for a spirit hath not flesh and bones, as ye see me have"— this same Jesus, with a material body, is to come in the clouds of heaven. In the same manner as He went up He shall come down. He shall be literally seen. The words cannot be honestly read in any other way.

"Every eye shall see him." Yes, I do literally expect to see my Lord with these eyes of mine, even as that saint expected who long ago fell asleep, believing that though the worms devoured his body, yet in his flesh he should see God, whom his eye should see for himself, and not another. There will be a real resurrection of the body, though the moderns doubt it: such a resurrection that we shall see Jesus with our own eyes. We shall not find ourselves in a shadowy, dreamy land of floating fictions, where we may perceive, but cannot see.

We shall not be airy nothings, mysterious, vague, impalpable; but we shall literally see our glorious Lord, whose appearing will be no phantom show, or shadow dance. Never day more real than the day of judgment; never sight more true than the Son of man upon the throne of His glory. Will you take this statement home, that you may feel the force of it? We are getting too far away from facts nowadays, and too much into the realm of myths and notions. "Every eye shall see him," in this there shall be no delusion.

Note well that *He is to be seen of all kinds of living men:* every eye shall see Him: the king and the peasant, the most learned and the most ignorant. Those that were blind before shall see when He appears. I remember a man born blind who loved our Lord most intensely, and he was wont to glory in this, that his eyes had been reserved for his Lord. Said he, "The first whom I shall ever see will be the Lord Jesus Christ. The first sight that greets my newly-opened eyes will be the Son of man in His glory."

There is great comfort in this to all who are now unable to behold the sun. Since "every eye shall see him," you also shall see the King in His beauty. Small pleasure is this to eyes that are full of filthiness and pride: you care not for this sight, and yet you must see it whether you please or do not please. You have hitherto shut your eyes to good things, but when Jesus comes you *must* see Him. All that dwell upon the face of the earth, if not at the same moment, yet with the same certainty, shall behold the once crucified Lord. They will not be able to hide themselves, nor to hide Him from their eyes. They will dread the sight, but it will come upon them, even as the sun shines on the thief who delights in the darkness. They will be obliged to own in dismay that they behold the Son of man: they will be so overwhelmed with the sight that there will be no denying it.

He will be seen of those who have been long since dead. What a sight that will be for Judas, and for Pilate, and for Caiaphas, and for Herod! What a sight it will be for those who, in their lifetime, said that there was no Saviour, and no need of one; or that Jesus was a mere man, and that His blood was not a propitiation for sin! Those that scoffed and reviled Him have long since died, but they shall all rise again, and rise to this heritage among the rest—that they shall see Him whom they blasphemed sitting in the clouds of heaven.

Prisoners are troubled at the sight of the judge. The trumpet of assize brings no music to the ears of criminals. But thou must hear it, O impenitent sinner! Even in thy grave thou must hear the voice of the Son of God, and live, and come forth from the tomb, to receive the things done in thy body, whether they be good or bad. Death cannot hide thee, nor the vault conceal thee, nor rottenness and corruption deliver thee. Thou art bound to see in thy body the Lord who will judge both thee and thy fellows.

It is mentioned here that *He will especially be seen by those that pierced Him.* In this is included all the company that nailed Him to the tree, with those that took the spear and made the gash in His side; indeed, all that had a hand in His cruel crucifixion. It includes all of these, but it comprehends many more besides. "They also who pierced him" are by no means a few. Who have pierced Him? Why those who once professed to love Him, and have gone back to the world. Those that once ran well, "What did hinder them?" And now they use their tongues to speak against the Christ whom once they professed to love. They also have pierced Him whose inconsistent lives have brought dishonor upon the sacred name of Jesus. They also have pierced Him, who refused His love, stifled their consciences, and refused His rebukes.

Alas, that so many of you should be piercing Him now by your base neglect of His salvation! They that went every Sunday to hear of Him, and that remained hearers only, destroying their own souls rather than yield to His infinite love: these pierced His tender heart. Dear hearers, I wish I could plead effectually with you tonight, so that you would not continue any longer among the number of those that pierced Him. If you will look at Jesus now, and mourn for your sin, He will put your sin away; and then you will not be ashamed to see Him in that day. Even though you did pierce Him, you will be able to sing, "Unto him that loved us, and washed us from our sins in his own blood." But, remember, if you persevere in piercing Him, and fighting against Him, you will still have to see Him in that day, to your terror and despair. He will be seen by you and by me, however ill we may behave. And what horror will that sight cost us!

I felt unfit to preach to you tonight; but last Lord's day I said that I would preach tonight if I could possibly manage it. It seemed barely impossible, but I could do no less than keep my word; and I also longed to be with you, for your sakes; for peradventure there may not remain many more occasions on which I shall be permitted to preach the gospel among you. I am often ill; who knows how soon I shall come to my end? I would use all that remains to me of physical strength and providential opportunity. We never know how soon we may be cut off, and then we are gone for ever from the opportunity of benefiting our fellow-men.

It were a pity to be taken away with one opportunity of doing good unused.

So would I earnestly plead with you under the shadow of this great truth: I would urge you to make ready, since we shall both behold the Lord in the day of His appearing. Yes, I shall stand in that great throng. You also will be there. How will you feel? You are not accustomed, perhaps, to attend a place of worship; but you will be there, and the spot will be very solemn to you. You may absent yourself from the assemblies of the saints, but you will not be able to absent yourself from the gathering of that day. You will be there, one in that great multitude; and you will see Jesus the Lord as truly as if you were the only person before Him, and He will look upon you as certainly as if you were the only one that was summoned to His bar.

Will you kindly think of all this as I close this second head? Silently repeat to yourself the words, "Every eye shall see him, and they also that pierced him."

III. And now I must close with the third head, which is a painful one, but needs to be enlarged upon: HIS COMING WILL CAUSE GREAT SORROW. What does the text say about His coming? "All kindreds of the earth shall wail because of Him."

"All kindreds of the earth." Then *this sorrow will be very general*. You thought, perhaps, that when Christ came, He would come to a glad world, welcoming Him with song and music. You thought that there might be a few ungodly persons who would be destroyed with the breath of His mouth, but that the bulk of mankind would receive Him with delight. See how different—"All kindreds of the earth," that is, all sorts of men that belong to the earth; all earth-born men, men out of all nations and kindreds and tongues shall weep and wail, and gnash their teeth at His coming. O sirs, this is a sad outlook! We have not smooth things to prophesy. What think you of this?

And, next, *this sorrow will be very great.* They shall *"wail."* I cannot put into English the full meaning of that most expressive word. Sound it at length, and it conveys its own meaning. It is as when men wring their hands and burst out into a loud cry; or as when eastern women, in their anguish, rend their garments, and lift up their voices with mournful notes. All the kindreds of the earth shall wail: wail as a mother laments over her dead child; wail as a man might wail who found himself hopelessly imprisoned and doomed to die.

Such will be the hopeless grief of all the kindreds of the earth at the sight of Christ in the clouds: if they remain impenitent, they shall not be able to be silent; they shall not be able to repress or conceal their anguish, but they shall wail, or openly give vent to their horror. What a sound that will be which will go up before high heaven when Jesus sits upon the cloud, and in the fulness of His power summons them to judgment! Then "they shall wail because of him."

Will your voice be heard in that wailing? Will your heart be breaking in that general dismay? How will you escape? If you are one of the kindreds of the earth, and remain impenitent, you will wail with the rest of them. Unless you now fly to Christ, and hide yourself in Him, and so become one of the kindred

of heaven—one of His chosen and blood-washed ones—
who shall praise His name for washing them from their
sins—unless you do this, there will be wailing at the
judgment seat of Christ, and you will be in it.

Note one more truth. It is quite certain that when
Jesus comes in those latter days *men will not be expecting great things of Him.* You know the talk they
have nowadays about "a larger hope." Today they
deceive the people with the idle dreams of repentance
and restoration after death, a fiction unsupported by
the least tittle of Scripture. If these kindreds of the
earth expected that when Christ would come they
would all die out and cease to be, they would rejoice
that thereby they had escaped the wrath of God.
Would not each unbeliever say, "It were a consummation devoutly to be wished"? If they thought that at
His coming there would be a universal restoration and
a general jail delivery of souls long shut up in prison,
would they wail? If Jesus could be supposed to come
to proclaim a general restoration they would not wail,
but shout for joy.

Ah, no! It is because His coming to the impenitent
is black with blank despair that they will wail because
of Him. If His first coming does not give you eternal
life, His second coming will not. If you do not hide
in His wounds when He comes as your Saviour, there
will be no hiding place for you when He comes as
your Judge. They will weep and wail because, having
rejected the Lord Jesus, they have turned their backs
on the last possibility of hope.

Why do they wail *because of Him?* Will it not be
because they will see Him in His glory, and they will
recollect that they slighted and despised Him? They

will see Him come to judge them, and they will remember that once He stood at their door with mercy
in His hands and said, "Open to me," but they would
not admit Him. They refused His blood: they refused
His righteousness: they trifled with His sacred name;
and now they must give an account for this wickedness.
They put Him away in scorn, and now, when He comes,
they find that they can trifle with Him no longer. The
days of child's-play and of foolish delay are over; and
now they have solemnly to give in their life's account.
See, the books are opened! They are covered with dis-
mays as they remember their sins, and know that they
are written down by a faithful pen. They must give an
account; and unwashed and unforgiven they cannot
render that account without knowing that the sentence
will be, "Depart, ye cursed." This is why they weep
and wail because of Him.

O souls, my natural love of ease makes me wish
that I could preach pleasant things to you; but they
are not in my commission. I need scarce wish, however,
to preach a soft gospel, for so many are already doing
it to your cost. As I love your immortal souls, I dare
not flatter you. As I shall have to answer for it in
the last great day, I must tell you the truth.

> "Ye sinners seek His face
> Whose wrath ye cannot bear."

Seek the mercy of God tonight. I have come here in
pain to implore you to be reconciled to God. "Kiss the
Son lest he be angry, and ye perish from the way, when
his wrath is kindled but a little. Blessed are all they
that put their trust in him."

But if you will not have my Lord Jesus, He comes
all the same for that. He is on the road now, and when

He comes you will wail because of Him. Oh that you would make Him your friend, and then meet Him with joy! Why will ye die? He gives life to all those who trust Him. Believe, and live.

God save your souls tonight, and He shall have the glory. Amen.

CHAPTER VII

JESUS ADMIRED IN THEM THAT BELIEVE

"When he shall come to be glorified in His saints, and to be admired in all them that believe (because our testimony among you was believed) in that day" (II Thessalonians 1:10).

WHAT A DIFFERENCE between the first and second coming of our Lord! When He shall come a second time it will be to be glorified and admired, but when He came the first time it was to be despised and rejected of men. He comes a second time to reign with unexampled splendor, but the first time He came to die in circumstances of shame and sorrow. Lift up your eyes, ye sons of light, and anticipate the change, which will be as great for you as for your Lord; for now ye are hidden even as He was hidden, and misunderstood when He walked among the sons of men. "We know that, when he shall appear, we shall be like him; for we shall see him as he is." His manifestation will be our manifestation, and in the day in which He is revealed in glory then shall His saints be glorified with Him.

Observe that our Lord is spoken of as coming in His glory, and as at the same time taking vengeance in flaming fire on them that know not God, and that obey not the gospel. This is a note of great terror to all those who are ignorant of God, and wickedly unbelieving concerning His Christ. Let them take heed, for the Lord will gain glory by the overthrow of His enemies, and those who would not bow before Him cheerfully shall be compelled to bow before Him abjectly: they shall crouch at His feet, they shall lick the dust in terror, and at the glance of His eyes they shall utterly wither away, as it is written, they "shall be punished with everlasting destruction from the presence of the Lord, and from the glory of His power."

But this is not the main object for which Christ will come, nor is this the matter in which He findeth His chiefest glory, for, observe, He does this as it were by the way, when He comes for another purpose. To destroy the wicked is a matter of necessity in which His spirit takes no delight, for He doth this, according to the text, not so much when He cometh to do it as when He shall come with another object, namely, "To be glorified in His saints, and to be admired in them that believe."

The crowning honor of Christ will be seen in His people, and this is the design with which He will return to this earth in the latter days, that He may be illustrious in His saints and exceedingly magnified in them. Even now His saints glorify Him. When they walk in holiness they do, as it were, reflect His light; their holy deeds are beams from Him who is the Sun of Righteousness. When they believe in Him they also glorify Him, for there is no grace which pays lowlier homage at the throne of Jesus than the grace of faith whereby we trust Him, and so confess Him to be our all in all.

We do glorify our gracious Lord, but, beloved brethren, we must all confess that we do not this as we could desire, for, alas, too often we dishonor Him, and grieve His Holy Spirit. By our want of zeal and by our many sins we are guilty of discrediting His gospel and dishonoring His name. Happy, happy, happy day when this shall no more be possible, when we shall be rid of the inward corruption which now worketh itself into outward sin, and shall never dishonor Christ again, but shall shine with a clear, pure radiance, like the moon on the Passover night, when it looketh the sun full in the face, and then shines upon the earth at her best. Today we are like vessels on the wheel, but half fashioned, yet even now somewhat of His divine skill is seen in us as His handiwork.

Still the unformed clay is in part seen, and much remains to be done; how much more of the great Potter's creating wisdom and sanctifying power will be displayed when we shall be the perfect products of His hand! In the bud and germ our new nature brings honor to its Author; it will do far more when its perfection manifests the Finisher. Then shall Jesus be glorified and admired in every one of us when the days of the new creation are ended and God shall usher in the eternal Sabbath by pronouncing His grace-work to be very good.

I. Let us consider carefully THE SPECIAL GLORIFICATION HERE INTENDED.

And the first point to note is *the time*. The text saith, "When he shall come to be glorified in his saints." The full glorification of Christ in His saints will be when He shall come a second time, according to the sure word of prophecy. He is glorified in them now, for He saith, "All mine are thine, and thine are mine; and I am glorified in them"; but as yet that glory is perceptible to Himself rather than to the outer world. The lamps are being trimmed, they will shine ere long.

These are the days of preparation before that Sabbath which is in an infinite sense a high day. As it was said of Esther, that for so many months she prepared herself with myrrh and sweet odors before she entered the king's palace, to be espoused of him, even so are we now being purified and made ready for that august day when the perfected church shall be presented unto Christ as a bride unto her husband. John saith of her that she shall be "prepared as a bride adorned for her husband."

This is our night, wherein we must watch, but behold the morning cometh, a morning without clouds, and then shall we walk in a seven-fold light because our Well-beloved hath come. That second advent of His will be His revelation: He was under a cloud here, and men perceived Him not save only a few who beheld His glory; but when He comes a second time all veils will be removed and every eye shall see the glory of His countenance. For this He waits and His church waits with Him. We know not when the set time shall arrive, but every hour is bringing it nearer to us, therefore let us stand with loins girt, awaiting it.

Note, secondly, *in whom* this glorification of Christ is to be found. The text does not say He will be glorified "by" His saints, but *"in* His saints." There is a shade of difference, yea, more than a shade, between the two terms. We endeavor to glorify Him now by our actions, but then He will be glorified in our persons, and character, and condition. He is glorified *by* what we do, but He is at last to be glorified *in* what we are. Who are these in whom Jesus is to be glorified and admired? They are spoken of under two descriptions: "in His saints," and "in all them that believe."

In "His saints" first. All those in whom Christ will be glorified are described as holy ones or saints: men and women who have been sanctified, and made pure, whose gracious lives show that they have been under the teaching of the Holy Spirit, whose obedient actions prove that they are disciples of a Holy Master, even of Him who was "holy, harmless, undefiled, and separate from sinners." But, inasmuch as these saints are also said to be believers, I gather that the holiness which will honor Christ at last is a holiness based on faith in Him, a holiness of which this was the root—that they first trusted in Christ, and then, being saved, they loved their Lord and obeyed Him. Their faith wrought by love and purified their souls, and so cleansed their lives. It is an inner as well as an outer purity, arising out of the living and operative principle of faith.

If any think that they can attain to holiness apart from faith in Christ they are as much mistaken as he who should hope to reap a harvest without casting seed into the furrows. Faith is the bulb, and saintship is the delightfully fragrant flower which cometh of it when planted in the soil of a renewed heart. Beware, I pray you, of any pretence to a holiness arising out of yourselves, and maintained by the energy of your own unaided wills; as well look to gather grapes of thorns or figs of thistles. True saintship must spring from confidence in the Saviour of sinners, and if it doth not it is lacking in the first elements of truth. How can that be a perfect character which finds its basis in self-esteem? How could Christ be glorified by saints who refuse to trust in Him?

I would call your attention once again to the second description, "All them that believe." This is enlarged by the hint that they are believers in a certain testimony, according to the bracketed sentence—"because our testimony among you was believed." Now, the testimony of the apostles was concerning Christ. They saw Him in the body, and they bore witness that He was "God manifest in the flesh"; they saw His holy life, and they bore witness to it; they saw His death of grief, and they witnessed that "God was in Christ reconciling the world unto Himself"; they saw Him risen from the dead, and they said, "We are witnesses of His resurrection"; they saw Him rise into heaven, and they bore witness that God had taken Him up to His right hand.

Now, all that believe this witness are saved. "If thou shalt confess with thy mouth the Lord Jesus, and shalt believe in thine heart that God hath raised him from the dead, thou shalt be saved." All who with a simple faith come and cast themselves upon the incarnate God, living and dying for men, and ever sitting at the right hand of God to make intercession for them —these are the people in whom Christ will be glorified and admired at the last great day. But inasmuch as they are first said to be saints, be it never forgotten that this faith must be a living faith, a faith which produces a hatred of sin, a faith which renews the character and shapes the life after the noble model of Christ, thus turning sinners into saints.

The two descriptions must not be violently rent asunder; you must not say that the favored people are sanctified without remembering that they are justified by faith, or may you say that they are justified by faith without remembering that without holiness no man shall see the Lord, and that at the last the people in whom Christ will be admired will be those holy ones who were saved by faith in Him.

The saints will also admire Christ in one another. As I shall see you and you shall see your brethren and sisters in Christ all perfect, you will be filled with wonderment, and gratitude, and delight. You will be free from all envy there, and therefore you will rejoice in all the beauty of your fellow saints: their heaven will be a heaven to you, and what a multitude of heavens you will have as you will joy in the joy of all the redeemed! We shall as much admire the Lord's handiwork in others as in ourselves, and shall each one praise Him for saving all the rest. You will see your Lord in all your brethren, and this will make you praise and adore Him world without end with a perpetual amazement of ever growing delight.

Then shall Satan and His defeated legions, and the lost spirits of ungodly men, bite their lips with envy and rage, and tremble at the majesty of Jesus in that day. By their confessed defeat and manifest despair they shall glorify Him in His people, in whom they have been utterly overthrown. They shall see that there is not one lost whom He redeemed by blood, not one snatched away of all the sheep His Father gave Him, not one warrior enlisted beneath His banner fallen in the day of battle, but all more than conquerors through Him that loved them. What despair shall seize upon diabolic spirits as they discover their entire defeat! Defeated in men who were once their slaves! Poor dupes whom they could so easily beguile by their craftiness—defeated even in these! Jesus triumphant by taking the lambs from between the lion's jaws, and rescuing His feeble sheep from their power, will utterly put them to shame in His redeemed. With what anguish will they sink into the hell prepared for them, because now they hear with anger all earth and heaven and every star ringing with the shout — Hallelujah, Hallelujah, Hallelujah, for the Lord God omnipotent reigneth, and the Lamb hath conquered by His blood.

You see then that there are enough spectators to magnify Christ in His saints; and so, let us inquire *in what degree* will the Lord Jesus be glorified? Our answer is, it will be to the very highest degree. He shall come to be glorified in His saints to the utmost, for this is clear from the words, "to be admired." When our translation was made the word "admired" had to ordinary Englishmen a stronger flavor of wonder than it has to us now. We often speak of admiring a thing in the softer sense of loving it, but the real meaning of the English word, and of the Greek also, is *wonder*: our Lord will be wondered at in all them that believe. Those who look upon the saints will feel a sudden wonderment of sacred delight; they will be startled with the surprising glory of the Lord's work in them; "We thought He would do great things, but this! This surpasseth conception!" Every saint will be a wonder to himself. "I thought my bliss would be great, but not like this!"

All His brethren will be a wonder to the perfected believer. He will say, "I thought the saints would be perfect, but I never imagined such a transfiguration of excessive glory would be put upon each of them. I could not have imagined my Lord to be so good and gracious." The angels in heaven will say that they never anticipated such deeds of grace: they did know that He had undertaken a great work, but they did

not know that He would do so much for His people
and in His people. This first-born sons of light, used
to great marvels from of old, will be entranced with
a new wonder as they see the handiwork of Immanuel's
free grace and dying love. The men who once despised
the saints, who called them canting hypocrites and
trampled on them, and perhaps slew them, the kings
and princes of the earth who sold the righteous for a
pair of shoes, what will they say when they see the
least of the Saviour's followers become a prince of
more illustrious rank than the great ones of the earth,
and Christ shining out in every one of these favored
beings? For their uplifting Jesus will be wondered at
by those who once despised both Him and them.

My next point leads us into the very bowels of the
subject; *in what respects* will Christ be glorified and
wondered at? I cannot expect to tell you one tenth
part of it. I am only going to give you a little sample
of what this must mean; exhaustive exposition were
quite impossible to me. I think with regard to His
saints that Jesus will be glorified and wondered at
on account of their number—"a number that no man
can number." John was a great arithmetician, and he
managed to count up to one hundred and forty-four
thousand of all the tribes of the children of Israel;
but that was only a representative number for the Jewish
church: as for the church of God, comprehending the
Gentile nations, he gave up all idea of computation,
and confessed that it is "a number which no man can
number." When he heard them sing he says, "I heard
a voice like the voice of many waters and like great
thunder." There were so many of them that their
song was like the Mediterranean sea lashed to fury

by a tempest, nay, not one great sea in uproar, but ocean upon ocean, the Atlantic and the Pacific piled upon each other, and the Arctic upon these, and other oceans upon these, layers of oceans, all thundering out their mightiest roar: and such will be the song of the redeemed, for the crowds which swell the matchless hymn will be beyond all reckoning.

Behold, and see, ye who laughed at His kingdom, see how the little one has become a thousand! Now look ye, ye foes of Christ, who saw the handful of corn on the top of the mountains; see how the fruit thereof doth shake like Lebanon, and they of the city do flourish like grass of the earth. Who can reckon the drops of the dew or the sands on the sea shore? When they have counted these then shall they not have guessed at the multitude of the redeemed that Christ shall bring to glory. And all this harvest from one grain of wheat, which except it had fallen into the ground and died would have remained alone! What said the word? "If it die, it shall bring forth much fruit." Is not the prophecy fulfilled? O beloved, what a harvest from the lone Man of Nazareth! What fruit from that glorious Man—the Branch! Men esteemed Him stricken, smitten of God and afflicted; and they made nothing of Him, and yet there sprang of Him (and He as good as dead) these multitudes which are many as the stars of heaven. Is He not glorified and wondered at in them? The day shall declare it without fail.

But there is quality as well as quantity. He is admired in His saints because they are every one of them proofs of His power to save from evil. My eye can hardly bear, even though it be but in imagination, to gaze upon the glittering ranks of the white-robed ones, where each one outshines the sun, and they are all as if a sevenfold midday had clothed them. Yet all these, as I look at them, tell me, "We have washed our robes—for they were once defiled. We have made them white—but this whiteness is caused by the blood of the Lamb." These were heirs of wrath even as others, these were dead in trespasses and sins; all these like sheep had gone astray and turned every one to his own way; but look at them and see how He has saved them, washed them, cleansed them, perfected them! His power and grace are seen in all of them.

If your eye will pause here and there you will discover some that were supremely stubborn, whose neck was as an iron sinew, and yet He conquered them by love. Some were densely ignorant, but He opened their blind eyes; some grossly infected with the leprosy of lust, but He healed them; some under Satan's most terrible power, but He cast the devil out of them. Oh, how He will be glorified in special cases! In yon drunkard made into a saint, in yon blasphemer turned into a loving disciple, in yon persecutor who breathed out threatening taught to sing everlastingly a hymn of praise! He will be exceedingly glorified in such. Brethren, beloved in the Lord, in each one of us there was some special difficulty as to our salvation, some impossibility which was possible with God, though it would have been for ever impossible with us.

Remember, also, that all those saints made perfect would have been in hell had it not been for the Son's atoning sacrifice. This they will remember the more vividly, because they will see other men condemned for the sins with which they also were once polluted. The

crash of vengeance upon the ungodly will make the
saints magnify the Lord the more as they see themselves delivered. They will each feel—

> "Oh, were it not for grace divine,
> The fate so dreadful had been mine."

In each one the memory of the horrible pit whence
they were drawn and the miry clay out of which they
were uplifted shall make their Saviour more glorified
and wondered at.

Perhaps the chief point in which Christ will be
glorified will be — the absolute perfection of all the
saints. They shall then be "without spot, or wrinkle,
or any such thing." We have not experienced what
perfection is, and therefore we can hardly conceive it;
our thoughts themselves are too sinful for us to get
a full idea of what absolute perfection must be; but,
dear brethren, we shall have no sin left in us, for they
are "without fault before the throne of God," and we
shall have no remaining propensity to sin. There shall
be no bias in the will towards that which is evil, but
it shall be fixed for ever upon that which is good. The
affections will never be wanton again, they will be
chaste for Christ. The understanding will never make
mistakes. You shall never put bitter for sweet, nor
sweet for bitter; you shall be "perfect, even as your
Father which is in heaven is perfect": and truly, brethren, He who worketh this in us will be a wonder. Christ
will be admired and adored because of this grand result.

O mighty Master, with what strange moral alchemy
didst Thou work to turn that morose dispositioned man
into a mass of love! How didst Thou work to lift that
selfish Mammonite up from his hoarded gains to make
him find his gain in Thee? How didst Thou overcome

that proud spirit, that fickle spirit that lazy spirit, that
lustful spirit—how didst Thou contrive to take all these
away? How didst Thou extirpate the very roots of sin,
and every little rootlet of sin, out of Thy redeemed,
so that not a tiny fibre can be found? "The sins of
Jacob shall be sought for and they shall not be found,
yea, they shall not be, saith the Lord." Neither the
guilt of sin nor the propensity of sin—both shall be
gone, and Christ shall have done it, and He will be
"glorified in His saints, and admired in them that believe."

This is but the beginning, however. There will be
seen in every saint, in that last wondrous day, the
wisdom and power and love of Christ in having
brought them through all the trials of the way. He
kept their faith alive when else it would have died
out: He sustained them under trials when else they
would have fainted; He held them fast in their in-
tegrity when temptation solicited them, and they had
almost slipped with their feet. Aye, He sustained some
of them in prison, and on the rack, and at the stake,
and held them faithful still!

One might hardly wish to be a martyr, but I reckon
that the martyrs will be the admiration of us all, or
rather Christ will be admired in them. However they
could bear such pain as some of them did endure for
Christ's sake none of us can guess, except that we
know that Christ was in them suffering in His members.
Eternally will Jesus be wondered at in them as all in-
telligent spirits shall see how He upheld them, so that
neither tribulation, nor distress, nor nakedness, nor
famine, nor sword, could separate them from His love.
These are the men that wandered about in sheep-skins

and goat-skins, destitute, afflicted, tormented, of whom the world was not worthy, but now they stand arrayed as kings and priests in surpassing glory for ever. Verily, their Lord shall be admired in them. Say you not so?

Recollect, dear friends, that we shall see in that day how the blessed Christ, as "Head over all things to His church," has ruled every providence to the sanctification of His people — how the dark days begat showers which made the plants of the Lord to grow, how the fierce sun which threatened to scorch them to the root, filled them with warmth of love divine and ripened their choice fruit. What a tale the saints will have to tell of how that which threatened to damp the fire of grace made it burn more mightily, how the stone which threatened to kill their faith was turned into bread for them, how the rod and staff of the Good Shepherd was ever with them to bring them safely home.

I have sometimes thought that if I get into heaven by the skin of my teeth I will sit down on the glory-shore and bless for ever Him who, on a board, or on a broken piece of the ship, brought my soul safe to land; and surely they who obtain an abundant entrance, coming into the fair havens, like a ship in full sail, without danger of shipwreck, will have to praise the Lord that they thus came into the blessed port of peace: in each case the Lord will be specially glorified and admired.

I cannot stop over this, but I must beg you to notice that as a king is glorious in his regalia, so will Christ put on His saints as His personal splendor in that day when He shall make up His jewels. It is with Christ as it was with that noble Roman matron who, when she called at her friends' houses and saw their trinkets, asked them to come next day to her house, and she would exhibit her jewels. They expected to see ruby, and pearl, and diamond, but she called in her two boys, and said, "These are my jewels."

Even so will Jesus instead of emerald and amethyst, and onyx and topaz, exhibit His saints. "These are My choice treasures," saith He, "in whom I will be glorified." Solomon surely was never more full of glory than when he had finished the temple, when all the tribes came together to see the noble structure, and confessed it to be "beautiful for situation, the joy of the whole earth." But what will be the glory of Christ when all the living stones shall be put into their places and His church shall have her windows of agates and her gates of carbuncle, and all her borders of precious stones. Then, indeed, will He be glorified, when the twelve foundations of His new Jerusalem shall be courses of stones most precious, the like of which was never seen.

Now, inasmuch as my text lays special stress upon *believing*, I invite you just for a minute to consider how as believers as well as saints the saved ones will glorify their Lord.

First, it will be wonderful that there should be so many brought to faith in Him: men with no God, and men with many gods, men steeped in ignorance, and men puffed up with carnal wisdom, great men and poor men, all brought to believe in the one Redeemer and praise Him for His great salvation. Will He not be glorified in their common faith? It will magnify Him that these will all be saved by faith, and not by

their own merits. Not one among them will boast that
he was saved by his own good works, but all of them
will rejoice to have been saved by that blessedly simple
way of "Believe and live," saved by sovereign grace
through the atoning blood, looked to by the tearful
eye of simple faith. This, too, shall make Jesus glorious, that all of them, weak as they were, were made
strong by faith; all of them personally unfit for battle
were yet made triumphant in conflict because by faith
they overcame through the blood of the Lamb. All
of them shall be there to show that their faith was
honored, that Christ was faithful to His promise, and
never allowed them to believe in vain. All of them
standing in heavenly places, saved by faith, will ascribe
every particle of the glory to the Lord Jesus only:—

> "I ask them whence their victory came?
>   They, with united breath,
> Ascribe their conquest to the Lamb,
>   Their triumph to His death."

They believed and were saved, but faith taketh no
credit to itself; it is a self-denying grace, and putteth
the crown upon the head of Christ, and therefore is it
written that He will be glorified in His saints, and He
will also be admired in all them that believe.

I have scarcely skirted the subject even now, and
time is failing me. I want you to reflect that Jesus will
be glorified in the risen bodies of all His saints. Now,
in heaven, they are pure spirits, but when He shall come
they shall be clothed again. Poor body, thou must
sleep awhile, but what thou shalt be at thine awaking
doth not yet appear. Thou art now the shrivelled seed,
but there is a flower to come of thee which shall be
lovely beyond all thought. Though sown in weakness,

this body shall be raised in power; though sown in corruption, it shall be raised in incorruption.

Weakness, weariness, pain, and death will be banished for ever; infirmity and deformity will be all unknown. The Lord will raise up our bodies to be like unto His glorious body. Oh, what a prospect lies before us! Let us remember that this blessed resurrection will come to us because He rose, for there must be a resurrection to the members because the Head has risen. Oh, the charm of being a risen man perfect in body, soul and spirit! All that charm will be due to Christ, and therefore He will be admired in us.

Then let us think of the absolute perfection of the church as to numbers: all who have believed in Him will be with Him in glory. The text saith, He will be "admired in *all* them that believe." Now, if some of those who believe perished He would not be admired in them, but they will all be there, the little ones as well as the great ones. You will be there, you poor feeble folk who when you say "Lord, I believe," are obliged to add "help Thou mine unbelief." He shall be admired in all believers without a single exception, and peradventure there shall be more wonder at the going to heaven of the weak believers than at the stronger ones. Mr. Greatheart, when he comes there will owe his victories to his Master and lay his laurels at His feet; but fainting Feeblemind, and limping Ready-to-halt with his crutches, and trembling Little-faith, when they enter into rest will make heaven ring with notes of even greater admiration that such poor creeping worms of the earth should win the day by mighty grace.

Suppose that one of them should be missing at last!

Stop the harps! Silence the songs! No beginning to be merry while one child is shut out! I am quite certain if as a family we were going to sing our evening hymn of joy and thankfulness, if mother said, "Where is the little mite? Where is the last one of the family?" there would be a pause. If we had to say—she is lost, there would be no singing and no resting till she was found. It is the glory of Jesus that as a Shepherd He has lost none of His flock; as the Captain of Salvation He has brought many sons to glory, and has lost none, and hence He is admired, not in some that believe, nor yet in all but one, but He is "admired in *all* them that believe."

Does not this delight you, you who are weak and trembling, that He will be admired in you? There is little to admire in you at present, as you penitently confess; but since Christ is in you now, and will be more fully manifested in you, there will ere long be much to admire. May you partake in the excellence of our divine Lord and be conformed to His likeness that He many be seen in you and glorified in you.

Another point of admiration will be the eternal safety of all His believing people. There they are, safe from fear of harm. Ye dogs of hell, you howled at their heels and hoped to devour them; but lo, they are clean escaped from you! What must it be to be lifted above gun-shot of the enemy, where no more watch shall need to be kept, for even the roar of the Satanic artillery cannot be heard? O glorious Christ, to bring them all to such a state of safety, Thou art indeed to be wondered at forever.

II. I have no time to make those SUGGESTIONS with

which I intended to have finished, and so I will just tell you what they would have been.

First, the text suggests that the principal subject for self-examination with us all should be—Am I a saint? Am I holy? Am I a believer in Christ? Yes or no, for on that yes or no must hang your glorification of Christ, or your banishment from His presence.

The next thing is—observe the small value of human opinion. When Christ was here the world reckoned Him to be nobody, and while His people are here they must expect to be judged in the same way. What do worldlings know about it? How soon will their judgment be reversed! When our Lord shall appear even those who sneered will be compelled to admire. When they shall see the glory of Christ in every one of His people, awe-stricken, they will have nothing to say against us; nay, not even the false tongue of malicious slander shall dare to hiss out a serpent word in that day. Never mind them, then; put up with reproach which shall so soon be silenced.

The next suggestion is a great encouragement to enquirers who are seeking Christ; for I put it to you, you great sinners, if Jesus is to be glorified in saved sinners, would He not be glorified indeed if He saved you? If He were ever to save such a rebel as you have been, would it not be the astonishment of eternity? I mean you who are known in the village as Wicked Jack, or known as a common swearer — what if my Master were to make a saint of you? Bad, raw material! Yet suppose He transformed you into a precious jewel, and made you to be as holy as God is holy, what would you say of Him? "Say of Him," say you, "I would praise Him world without end." Yes, and you shall do so if you will come and trust Him. Put your trust in Him. The Lord help you to do so at once, and He shall be admired even in you for ever and ever.

Our text gives an exhortation to believers also. Will Jesus Christ be honored and glorified in all the saints? Then let us think well of them all, and love them all. Some dear children of God have uncomely bodies, or they are blind or deformed, or maimed; and many of these have scanty purses, and it may be the church knows most of them as coming for alms: moreover, they have little knowledge, little power to please, and they are uncouth in manners, and belong to what are called the lowest ranks of society: do not, therefore, despise them, for one day our Lord will be glorified in them. How He will be admired in yonder poor bedridden woman when she rises from the workhouse to sing Hallelujah to God and the Lamb among the brightest of the shining ones. Why, methinks the pain, the poverty, the weakness, and the sorrow of saints below will greatly glorify the Captain of their Salvation as they tell how grace helped them to bear their burdens and to rejoice under their afflictions.

Lastly, brethren, this text ought to encourage all of you who love Jesus to go on talking about Him to others and bearing your testimony for His name. You see how the apostle Paul has inserted a few words by way of parenthesis. Draw the words out of the brackets, and take them home, "Because our testimony among you was believed." Do you see those crowds of idolatrous heathen, and do you see those hosts of saved ones before the throne? What is the medium which linked the two characters? By what visible means did the sinners become saints? Do you see that insignificant looking man with weak eyes? That man whose bodily presence is weak and whose speech is contemptible? Do you not see his bodkin and needle case? He has been making and mending tents, for he is only a tent-maker. Now, those bright spirits which shine like suns, flashing forth Christ's glory, were made thus bright through the addresses and prayers of that tent-maker. The Thessalonians were heathens plunged in sin, and this poor tent-maker came in among them and told them of Jesus Christ and His gospel; His testimony was believed; that belief changed the lives of his hearers and made them holy, and they being renewed came at length to be perfectly holy, and there they are, and Jesus Christ is glorified in them.

Beloved, will it not be a delightful thing throughout eternity to contemplate that you went into your Sunday-school class this afternoon, and you were afraid you could not say much, but you talked about Jesus Christ with a tear in your eye, and you brought a dear girl to believe in His saving name through your testimony. In years to come that girl will be among those that shine out to the glory of Christ for ever. Or you will get away this evening, perhaps, to talk in a lodging-house to some of those poor, despised tramps; you will go and tell one of those poor vagrants, or one of the fallen women, the story of your Lord's love and blood, and the poor broken heart will catch at the gracious word, and come to Jesus, and then a heavenly character will be begun, and another jewel secured for the Redeemer's diadem. Methinks you will admire His crown all the more because, as you see certain stones sparkling in it, you will say, "Blessed be His name for ever: He helped me to dive into the sea and find that pearl for Him," and now it adorns His sacred brow. Now, get at it, all of you! You that are doing nothing for Jesus, be ashamed of yourselves, and ask Him to work in you that you may begin to work for Him, and unto God shall be the glory, for ever and ever. Amen and Amen.

Printed in the United States of America